Cultivating Culture

Cultivating Culture

Creating Spirit-Powered Churches for the Future

Spencer Shaw

ISBN 9798218452810

Published by Thinking Theologically
thinkingtheologically.org

Cover Design: Oladimeji
Copy editor: Paul Higgins

To all the church leaders seeking to faithfully follow Jesus and trying to figure out how to fully embody what it means to be the church.

Table of Contents

Introduction

No matter what metrics you use, the church in America is struggling. More than 4,000 churches close their doors yearly, while only 1,000 new churches start.[1] In 2020, only 47% of Americans said they belonged to a church, synagogue, or mosque.[2] In the past twenty years, the percentage of Americans who do not identify with any religion has grown from 8% to 21%.[3] America is not only struggling with a Christian or church problem; it is struggling with a religion problem. Fewer and fewer people consider themselves religious as the numbers in churches, synagogues, and mosques continue to dwindle.

Such is especially the case among younger generations: 66% of adults born before 1946 belong to a church, while only 36% of millennials belong.[4] Only 34% of young adults who regularly attended church growing up continue to attend as adults.[5] Gen Z is the first generation where

---

[1] Richard J. Krejcir, "Statistics and Reasons for Church Decline," available at churchleadership.org/?articleid=42346.

[2] Jeffrey M. Jones, "U.S. Church Membership Falls Below Majority for First Time," Gallup.com, March 29, 2021, available at news.gallup.com/poll/341963/church-membership-falls-below-majority-first-time.aspx.

[3] Ibid.

[4] Ibid.

[5] Gallup, "In U.S., Childhood Churchgoing Habits Fade in Adulthood," Gallup.com, December 21, 2022, available at news.gallup.com/poll/467354/childhood-churchgoing-habits-fade-adulthood.aspx.

'nones' (48%) outnumber Christians (36%).[6] Religions, and churches in particular, have failed to engage and maintain younger generations, even those who group up in our churches.

However, this does not appear to be because younger generations, such as Gen Z, are entirely opposed to organized religion or spirituality. About 23% of Gen Z are weekly attendees at a religious gathering, which is higher than both Gen X and Millennials.[7] Research suggests that Gen Z desires authenticity and community. They are "starving for something that feels genuine." Gen Z is also highly motivated by social justice, and so they seek out religious groups and organizations that align with their values and through which they can pursue justice.[8]

The public scandals and abuses among many prominent churches compound the issues of church decline. Across all religious institutions, statistics show that sexual abuse by trusted leaders is a widespread and systemic issue.[9] Within the Catholic church, more than 6,000 clergy

---

[6] Ryan P. Burge, "Gen Z and Religion in 2021," *Religion in Public* (blog), June 15, 2022, available at religioninpublic.blog/2022/06/15/gen-z-and-religion-in-2021/.

[7] Ibid.

[8] ChurchTrac, "Gen Z and Religion: How Churches Can Reach Generation Z in 2024," ChurchTrac, available at churchtrac.com/articles.

[9] Peter Janci, "Church Sexual Abuse Statistics: Understanding the Prevalence Abuse," *Crew Janci LLP: Sexual Abuse Attorneys* (blog), May 24, 2023, available at crewjanci.com/church-sexual-abuse-statistics/.

members have been credibly accused of sexual abuse.[10] A 2022 investigation revealed that about 700 people, most of them children, were abused by Southern Baptist Church leaders and staff.[11]

The data suggests that churches are declining, but it is not primarily the fault of younger generations. Many churches and church leaders want to blame "kids these days" for their declining congregations. They believe that younger generations don't want to have anything to do with God and don't feel like they need God in their lives. They blame parents for not raising their children in "the faith." They blame a culture that is filled with individualism, that places a cell phone with endless internet and social media connections in everyone's hand, and has moved away from Christian values and ethics. They blame the school system, teachers, and "liberal" universities. The problems present in our churches are never the church's fault; they are everyone else's fault.

While some of these evaluations may contain some merit, overall, churches have been pointing the finger at the wrong culprit. Younger generations desire a spiritual connection, with 40% of Gen Z identifying as "spiritual but not religious."[12] Younger generations desire social justice that cares for the marginalized, abused, and poor, something that was at the core of the ministry of Jesus as presented in the

---

[10] Ron Meneo, "Catholic Church Priest Abuse | Sexual Abuse Scandal & Cover-Up," AbuseLawsuit.com, May 11, 2023, available at abuselawsuit.com/church-sex-abuse/.

[11] Janci, "Church Sexual Abuse Statistics."

[12] Jannik Lindner, "Gen Z Religion Statistics and Trends in 2024 • Gitnux," available at gitnux.org/gen-z-religion-statistics/.

Gospels. Younger generations attend church more frequently; they merely desire churches that resist abuses of power, the sexual abuse and exploitations of young and powerless people, and have a deep connection with the Christian tradition.

The values that younger generations are searching for were central to the lives of the earliest followers of Jesus. They are values that ought to be central in the cultures of modern-day churches but somehow have fallen out of the lives of many congregations. Churches should be places people can attend to pursue social justice. Churches should care for and stand up for the rights of the poor, abused, marginalized, such as refugees. Churches should be the last place that abuses of power and sexual abuse take place. Churches should provide people with a spiritual experience of the divine, connected to 2,000 years of Christian tradition and spiritual disciplines. However, it seems that people have been unable to find these values in their churches and have sought them elsewhere.

The American church's problem is not the fault of "kids these days" or American culture; it is the fault of the church. We are the reason that churches and religion are declining in our country. It is not because of the people "out there"; it is because of the people within our churches. The problem is not that people or the culture have changed, though both have, but that churches have changed. Churches no longer stand for the values or operate like they once did for the way of Jesus and his ministry.

If the modern church is to have any hope moving into the future, churches must undergo significant cultural changes. The church must change its culture before it can begin changing our world's culture. However, churches need to understand that the need for cultural change in our churches is not to attract younger people. The purpose of the church is not to attract outsiders by appealing to their desires, for the Gospel teaches us that we don't always desire the right thing. The purpose of the church is to glorify God and be a light to the world. The church attracts outsiders by providing a different way of doing life that doesn't give in to all human desires but transforms those desires by giving life meaning in light of how God created and designed human beings to reflect his image.

Churches don't need to change their culture to attract people; they need to change their culture to be more like Christ. Churches need to change their culture to tap into the immeasurable power of the Holy Spirit rather than relying on their own power and marketing tools. Churches need to change their culture to be the church, and as a result, we will attract younger people and set the church on a path of success moving into the future. People are not searching for earthly churches; they are searching for churches powered by the Holy Spirit and set on a path of participation in God's worldwide story.

With these thoughts in mind, this book seeks to aid churches in cultivating a church culture that allows the Holy Spirit to empower them to be active participants in God's worldwide story moving into the future. The approach of this book is not to tap into the most recent leadership models, organizational structures, or marketing techniques—though I believe, in certain instances, that these can be helpful tools for churches. Instead, this book seeks to go down to the foundation of church culture. In this book, we will allow the Spirit to speak to church culture directly by letting Scripture be our guide.

In the subsequent chapters, we will look at the types of cultures that the Apostle Paul sought to cultivate in the various churches he was involved with. What type of culture did Paul cultivate in Rome, Corinth, Galatia, Ephesus, Philippi, Colossae, Thessalonica, and through his Pastoral Epistles? We will consider the ins and outs of how Paul helped his churches cultivate Spirit-powered church cultures that pushed them to fully participate in what God was doing in the world. However, the goal of this book is not merely to present some theological principles of church culture but to bring those principles down to earth and apply them to the real life of real churches. Therefore, each chapter will also include some examples and helpful suggestions for applying Paul's principles in your church context to transform your church culture into a Spirit-powered culture actively participating in God's story.

Before we embark on our journey through Paul's letters, two additional things must be mentioned. First, throughout this book, I will use the language of a church "actively participating in God's worldwide story." This concept will be heavily developed in chapter 4, but a brief explanation of the phrase is necessary before we continue. Every person lives based on a story. How they understand themselves, others, the world, where they've come from, and where they're going make up their story. The decisions a person makes, what they believe is right and wrong, and what they believe is open to them is determined by their story.

God's interactions with his creation tell a story that is witnessed through Scripture. God's story explains where we came from (i.e., God created us; Gn 1–2). It explains where we are going (i.e., the new creation; Rv 21). It explains who we are—human beings created in the image of God (Gn 1:26–27). It explains right and wrong (i.e., the fruit of the Spirit; Gal 5:22–23). This story is worldwide because it encompasses God's entire creation, for God plans to redeem the entire creation.

Every person, a follower of Jesus or not, is a part of God's story because God will ultimately get his way; the story will end the same way regardless of what any individual does. However, one can choose to actively participate in God's story. That is, one can define one's life by God's story rather than another story. One can choose to live as an image-bearer of God and pursue the fruit of the Spirit, bringing the new creation of heaven to earth, and spread God's redeeming love, grace, and mercy everywhere they can.

I believe this summarizes God's calling for every church that claims to be followers of Jesus Christ. Every church is meant to be an active participant in God's worldwide story. As this book will explain, how individual churches participate in God's story differs by context. However, the overall calling for every Spirit-powered church is to fully and actively participate in God's worldwide story.

Second, the Christian tradition in which I was raised and minister is the Church of Christ, which has its roots in the Restoration Movement. Therefore, many of my observations and suggestions are drawn from my life and ministry within this tradition. However, I believe this book's observations are helpful for Christian traditions outside of my Church of Christ heritage. I believe this, first, because I seek to draw them first from Scripture and then from my tradition, though I recognize that no human can achieve this perfectly. Second, while there is great variety within the Christian tradition, there is also remarkable similarity. As Paul says, "There is one body and one Spirit, just as you were called to the one hope of your calling, one Lord, one faith, one baptism, one God and Father of all, who is above all and through all and in all" (Eph 4:4–6).

With that said, I recognize that not everything mentioned in this book will directly apply to every church context or tradition. The suggestions and applications in the following chapters are not lifelong principles; they are contextual applications based on personal experiences and observations. Therefore, feel free to take what works for you, change what needs to be changed, and leave the rest for those it may benefit. Every minister, church leader, and Christian must take the principles Paul applied to his church cultures and discern, through prayer and the Spirit, how those principles may best be applied in your church, tradition, and context. Cultivating culture is not a one-size-fits-all scheme or a one-time implementation. Cultivating culture is a lifelong process done by Spirit-filled people in individual contexts and churches as they seek to be active participants in God's worldwide story.

1

The Power of Culture

A Definition of Culture

If we are going to successfully discuss cultivating Spirit-powered church cultures for the future, then we must begin with a working definition of culture. I'm sure you've heard the term "culture" before and have used it in your own vocabulary. If you turn on the news or get on social media, you'll hear people discussing Christian culture versus secular culture or liberal culture versus conservative culture. People even argue about the dangers of culture seeping into our schools, churches, and homes.

Despite the pervasive use of the word "culture," it doesn't appear people know what this word means. In my experience, most people use the term "culture" as a catchall word for everything they don't like or agree with. "Christian culture is bad because …" "The liberal culture that is now taught in our schools is harming young people because …" As a result, the word "culture" has received a negative connotation in America, oddly enough because American culture has given it this negative connotation.

Wikipedia (yes, I recognize it's not the most reliable source, but I think it is helpful in this situation) defines culture as the "social behavior, institutions, and norms" of a particular nation or group of people. Consider American culture as an example. In America, certain social behaviors are acceptable, and others are unacceptable. For example, it is unacceptable to murder someone. It is acceptable, and even expected, that you tip your waiter or waitress at a restaurant (though tipping culture is getting a little out of hand!). American culture has important institutions that influence life in America (e.g., states, governments, schools, and churches). It is impossible to live in America and not be influenced, one way or another, by these institutions. Most Americans were educated in the American school system and have some connection to a religious institution, even if they no longer consider themselves religious. America also has norms or normal ways of doing life. The celebration of holidays would be an example of a social norm. A normal way of doing life in America is to grill food in celebration of the Fourth of July, a uniquely American holiday.

Wikipedia goes on to say that these aspects of culture influence individuals in those cultures by influencing their "knowledge, beliefs, arts, laws, customs, capabilities, and habits." In the American school system, history is usually taught in a way that presents America in a positive light. For example, Christopher Columbus is presented purely positively, though most Native Americans would have a different opinion. American laws, such as speed limits, are a unique part of American culture (try driving in Europe or India and you will quickly notice the cultural difference).

Culture also influences human capabilities, something most people don't realize. American culture has created the mythical "American Dream." The belief that people can do whatever they want if they put their mind to it is a sentiment that is not present in most cultures. Most other cultures do not tell their members that they can do anything if they work hard enough, so many people come to America to pursue their dreams because American culture tells them they can. Therefore, children growing up in America might be able to accomplish more than children growing up in another culture because American culture makes them believe they have the capability to do more.

In other words, everything that we do, think, or say is influenced by culture. Even language, the meaning we give to certain sounds, is 100% a cultural invention! Without a culture giving meaning to our words, all we would do is make unrecognizable sounds. In *Misreading Scripture with Western Eyes*, Randy Richards tells a story about how the same word can mean quite different things in different cultures. A pastor from Georgia was visiting Scotland. When he and his wife were getting into the car of a friend who was a British New Testament scholar, before getting into the vehicle, the pastor's wife said, "I'm going to plant my fanny right here in this seat," to which the British scholar was aghast since "fanny" is a very inappropriate word for the British![1]

Even if we choose to go against the cultural norms, our actions are still a response to culture. For example, in American culture, it is a norm to sleep around before

---

[1] "Fanny" in Britain refers specifically to female private parts. E. Randolph Richards and Brandon O'Brien, *Misreading Scripture with Western Eyes* (Downers Grove, IL: InterVarsity Press, 2013), 25.

marriage.[2] As Christians, we might choose to reject this cultural norm. While our actions may not match our culture, our choice to react against the culture is still influenced by culture. When we actively make the decision not to give in to the sexual pressures in our culture or when we decide to speak about sexual ethics in our churches, we are reacting against and, therefore, influenced by our culture.

So, living outside and unaffected by one's culture is impossible!

I want to add one more definition of culture. The sociology department at Texas A&M University defines culture as "a way of life of a group of people—the behaviors, beliefs, values, and symbols that they accept, generally without thinking about them, and that are passed along by communication and imitation from one generation to the next." Culture is the "way of life" for any group of people. American culture is the way of life for Americans. A church culture is the way of life for the members of that church. It is how the people who make up any group live in relation to each other. It is the values and symbols that mean something to

---

[2] The rate of premarital sex in the United States has remained steady since the 1950s, with roughly 95% of Americans having sex before marriage. Lawrence B. Finer, "Trends in Premarital Sex in the United States, 1954–2003," *Public Health Reports* 122, no. 1 (2007): 73–78; Guttmacher Institute, "Premarital Sex Is Nearly Universal Among Americans, And Has Been for Decades," March 1, 2016, available at guttmacher.org/news-release/2006/premarital-sex-nearly-universal-among-americans-and-has-been-decades.

them. In American culture, we might think of the value of hard work and the symbols of the American flag or Statue of Liberty. In church culture, we have the values of grace and mercy and the symbol of a cross.

As has been shown, the critical aspect of culture is that these values and symbols only mean something within a specific culture. The American flag might mean freedom and liberty to Americans, but oppression and cultural infiltration to a culture in the Middle East. A cross meant humiliation and defeat in the Roman Empire, but to followers of Jesus, it means power and victory.

Notice that this definition of culture states that culture is generally accepted by the people in that culture "without thinking about" it. Culture is in the air we breathe and the water we drink. There is no way of escaping culture! This also means it is challenging to change a bad culture. Since we accept culture without thinking about it, most people cannot define their culture. Their culture becomes a part of who they are. For example, American culture is individualistic and consumeristic. Nobody has to teach a child to want stuff verbally or that their opinions and feelings matter. It is ingrained in them by our culture.

The fact that we accept culture without thinking about it connects to how culture is passed along. Sometimes, culture is taught. For example, when children are taught history in school, it is taught in a way that enforces certain cultural norms. These are historical events we want to copy, and these are bad moments in history we do not want to repeat. Laws are also a part of a culture that are taught. In American culture, when a child turns 16, they can get their driver's license. However, before being issued a license, they must take a driver's education course to learn the cultural laws of America. The traffic laws in America differ from those in other cultures. For example, Americans drive on the right side of the road while Europeans drive on the left.

Other times, culture is passed on through "imitation." This is why you don't have to teach a child to desire things; they see it modeled for them every day by everybody. Another example is tipping. A child who grows up watching their parents tip the waiter every time they go to a restaurant likely will never need someone to teach them that they should tip. When they become adults, they naturally tip because that is what they believe you're supposed to do. Therefore, culture is a very powerful thing. Culture, generally without us even knowing, teaches us how to talk, think, behave, and what to value.

The Power of Culture

Though culture has received a negative connotation in America (the negative connotation being influenced by American culture), culture is not inherently evil. Culture is neutral. A culture can be evil, but a culture can also be good. Different aspects of a single culture might be good, while others are bad. There is generally a tension within a single culture between the aspects of that culture that are good and the ones that are bad.

In American culture, you might say that our consumeristic mentality is a negative aspect of our culture while the fact that we have traffic laws stating that everyone can't drive however they want as they can in other cultures is a good part of American culture.

Positive Culture

Let me give some examples of the power of positive culture. The **University of Alabama football team** has won six national championships over the past fourteen years. Under their now-retired head coach, Nick Saban, Alabama has not always had the best team or player. Some years they have, but other years they have not. Yet they have a chance to win a national championship every year. The reason is that Nick Saban created a winning culture. He brings in players and coaches who perpetuate and teach this culture. He has expectations for everyone based on this culture, from the coaches, to the players, to the equipment managers. The way that Alabama's players and coaches think, prepare, act, and play are all determined by their winning culture, and that is why Alabama can beat teams that are more talented than them but do not have the same winning culture. Saban says this about Alabama's culture: "You know, this is not a democracy. Everybody doesn't get to do what they want to do. Everybody doesn't get to do what they feel like doing. You've got to buy in and do what you're supposed to do to be a part of the team and do the things you need to do in practice."[3]

---

[3] Brian Dodd, "'This Is NOT A Democracy' and 5 Lessons on Creating a Winning Culture From Nick Saban's Epic Rant," *Brian Dodd on Leadership* (blog), August 22, 2021, available at briandoddonleadership.com/2021/08/22/this-is-not-a-democracy-and-5-lessons-on-creating-a-winning-culture-from-nick-sabans-epic-rant/.

McDonald's. Ray Croc, the founder of McDonald's as a small hamburger restaurant, had a famous saying, "If you have time to lean, you have time to clean." He created a culture with a specific work ethic, standards, and expectations. This is why McDonalds now has 40,275 restaurants worldwide[4] and is the largest U.S. chain with $25 billion in revenue.[5] It is not because McDonald's has the best hamburger; it is because of its culture.

Chick-fil-A. If you have ever been to Chick-fil-A, then you know that they have an amazing culture. I have never met a rude Chick-fil-A employee. It seems like every few months they are on the news because an employee saved someone from a kidnapping or delivered a baby in the restaurant, leaving me wondering where in the world they find these employees! I heard a story from Rick Warren, former pastor at Saddleback church in California. He was having lunch one day at Taco Bell with S. Truett Cathy, founder of Chick-fil-A. They had just been at the building site of a new Chick-fil-A, and when they got to Taco Bell, they both went into the bathroom to wash their hands. After washing their hands, Cathy got a paper towel and cleaned the bathroom sink. Warren asked him what he was doing, to which Cathy replied, "We teach our employees at Chick-fil-A to always leave a place better than they found it." Chick-fil-A has a

---

[4] Abby McCain, "22 McDonald's Statistics [2023]: Restaurant Counts, Facts, And Trends," *Zippia* (blog), March 21, 2023, available at zippia.com/advice/mcdonalds-statistics/.

[5] MacroTrends, "McDonald's Revenue 2010-2024," available at macrotrends.net/stocks/charts/MCD/mcdonalds/revenue#.

culture, which is why they are the third-largest U.S. chain with $21.58 billion in sales.[6]

Disney, one of the most well-known brands in the world. Did you know that at their parks, employees go through the park every night after closing and not only pick up trash but also repaint? It is literally a new park every morning. Disney has a culture. That is why all their parks combined have an average of 290,000 visitors daily![7]

Here's an important point about all these fantastic cultures: most people in these cultures would not be as good on their own. Players at Alabama are better at Alabama than at other schools because the culture makes them better. Workers at Chick-fil-A probably wouldn't deliver a baby if they were working at another restaurant because Chick-fil-A places people in a culture that makes them better people without them even knowing. Workers at Disney would not care so much about a park if Disney's culture did not instill it in them.

---

[6] Alicia Kelso, "Chick-Fil-A Continues to Gain Market Share While Setting Another Average Unit Volume Record," Nation's Restaurant News, April 4, 2024, available at nrn.com/quick-service/chick-fil-continues-gain-market-share-while-setting-another-average-unit-volume-record.

[7] Lisa Gilmore, "How Many People Go To Disney World Every Day?," *AllEars.Net* (blog), June 1, 2023, available at allears.net/2023/06/01/how-many-people-go-to-disney-world-every-day/. It is true that Disney's stock has dropped in recent years, perhaps signifying a drop in their overall culture. However, it was Disney's original culture that established it as an iconic company.

Here's another important point: when people step into these cultures for the first time, most of them don't like it. Going to play football at Alabama is a major culture shock for a player used to playing at their local high school. It is an entirely different standard. However, over time, they come to not only accept the new culture and realize its benefits but to expect the new culture. Slowly, everything in their lives begins to be defined by their new cultural expectations. They become new people.

Bad Cultures (Israel)

Culture is powerful, not only for the good, but it can also be powerful for the bad. Take the nation of Israel as an example. The people of Israel were in captivity in Egypt for around 400 years. During that time, they naturally picked up the culture of Egypt. So, when Moses leads them out of Egypt to Mt. Sinai, it is not long before they build an idol (i.e., the golden calf). As they say, "You can take the people out of Egypt, but you can't take Egypt out of the people." Israel continued to live based on the culture they had grown comfortable with. They were so used to all the other gods that surrounded them in Egypt that when they became discouraged and wondered where Yahweh had gone, they turned to another god.

Eventually, the people get turned around, and God, through the leadership of Moses and Joshua, began cultivating a new culture in Israel. God gives Israel the law, the standard for their new culture. Speaking of the law, Moses says in Deuteronomy 11:18–21:

You shall put these words of mine in your heart and soul, and you shall bind them as a sign on your hand, and fix them as an emblem on your forehead. Teach them to your children, talking about them when you are at home and when you are away, when you lie down and when you rise. Write them on the doorposts of your house and on your gates, so that your days and the days of your children may be multiplied in the land that the Lord swore to your ancestors to give them, as long as the heavens are above the earth.[8]

By following the law, Israel is to create a new culture and pass on this culture to future generations by both teaching and modeling.

However, the new culture only partially took. Following the leadership of Joshua comes the time of the judges, which is defined in this way in Judges 2:16–19:

Then the Lord raised up judges, who delivered them out of the power of those who plundered them. Yet they did not listen even to their judges; for they lusted after other gods and bowed down to them. They soon turned aside from the way in which their ancestors had walked, who had obeyed the commandments of the Lord; they did not follow their example. Whenever the Lord raised up judges for them, the Lord was

---

[8] All biblical citations are from the NRSV unless otherwise noted.

with the judge, and he delivered them from the hand of their enemies all the days of the judge; for the Lord would be moved to pity by their groaning because of those who persecuted and oppressed them. But whenever the judge died, they would relapse and behave worse than their ancestors, following other gods, worshiping them and bowing down to them. They would not drop any of their practices or their stubborn ways.

In many ways, you could say that Egypt was never fully taken out of the people. This shows the power of culture. No matter what happened, what God did, or how good a judge was at leading the people, the culture of idolatry and injustice perpetuated among the Israelite people continued to haunt them for the rest of their existence.

Church Culture

Not only do countries, sports teams, and businesses have cultures, so do churches. Every group of people, including the assembly of followers of Jesus called the church, has a culture. A church can choose, through their actions and words, to cultivate a good culture like Alabama or Chick-fil-A, empowering the church to be the people God has called and created them to be, or they can cultivate a bad culture, dooming them to a future much like the nation of Israel.

According to Scot McKnight, in his book *A Church Called Tov*, church cultures are formed through the relationship between four things: the church's narrative, acting out the Christian life, teaching the Christian faith, and articulating policies.[9]

Cultivating a church culture begins with church leaders (e.g., pastors, elders, deacons, ministers, teachers). Church leaders tell the church's narrative. What is our story? Where have we come from? Where are we going? What is our vision? Leaders act out the Christian life for others to see, passing on the culture through imitation. Leaders teach the Christian faith, passing on the culture through communication. Leaders articulate policies. How will the church operate? How will we deal with certain situations? What will we as a church do and get involved in, and what will we not?

However, a church culture does not rest solely on the shoulders of church leaders. The church congregation must accept the culture. The congregation reshapes the church's narrative as it begins to live out the narrative moving into the future. The congregation acts out the Christian life for the church, community, and world to see. The congregation reteaches the Christian faith to their children, families, friends, and community. The congregation rearticulates the church policies by acting on those set in place by church leaders.

Every single church member has a role in cultivating a church's culture. If any of the pieces fail, if leaders fail to lead a good culture, or if a congregation fails to live out a good culture, a church cannot cultivate a Spirit-powered

---

[9] Scot McKnight, *A Church Called Tov: Forming a Goodness Culture That Resists Abuses of Power and Promotes Healing* (Carol Stream, IL: Tyndale Elevate, 2020).

culture that will propel it into the future and transform it into the church God created it to be.

This is because we both form and are formed by church cultures. The things we do and say form a church culture, but the church culture, in turn, forms those who are part of that culture. A church culture changes the members into people who conform to and accept the culture, many times without people even knowing.

For example, if even a tiny part of a church begins to gossip unchecked, the whole church quickly begins to gossip, even people who have never gossiped before. The people who started gossiping formed a church culture of gossip. That church culture of gossip then formed the other members into people who conform to and accept the culture by turning them into gossipers.

This is why church culture is so influential. Yet most churches never consider what type of culture they cultivate. Every church has a culture, and everything said and done in a church contributes to cultivating that culture and shaping the members to conform to it. From the announcements you make, to the way you take care of the church building, to the things preached, to the way you handle conflict, everything helps to create and reinforce a church culture.

Churches must begin asking the question, what type of culture are we cultivating? What type of culture do our words and actions help to cultivate? Are we cultivating a good, Spirit-powered culture or another type of culture? A church can only be as successful in its role in God's story as the church culture it creates, and a church can only create a

Spirit-powered culture by every single member buying in and actively cultivating a Christ-centered, Spirit-powered culture.

Conclusion

I want to conclude with an illustration of the power of culture. In chapter 9 of *Atomic Habits*, James Clear tells the story of László Polgár.[10] Polgár is a Hungarian chess teacher, educational psychologist, and the father of the famous Polgár sisters: Zsuzsa, Zsófia, and Judit. László did not believe in innate ability but in the power of hard work. His mantra was that a genius is not born but is educated and trained.

László put his beliefs to the test by experimenting on his children. He believed that through the right culture of chess education and training, he could make his children into chess prodigies, regardless of their natural abilities. He homeschooled his children and filled the house with books and photos of chess and famous chess players. The children constantly competed against each other and in chess tournaments, and the family kept records of every person the children competed against.

László's oldest daughter, Zsuzsa, began playing chess at four years old and was winning against adult competition within six months. Zsófia, the middle daughter, was a world champion by age fourteen and, within a few years, became a grandmaster. The youngest, Judit, was beating her father by age five; by age twelve, she was the youngest to be named among the top 100 best chess players in the world; at fifteen

---

[10] James Clear, *Atomic Habits: An Easy & Proven Way to Build Good Habits & Break Bad Ones* (New York: Avery, 2018).

years and four months old, she became the youngest grandmaster of all time. For twenty-seven years, she was the world's top-ranked female chess player.

The Polgár sisters did not have a typical childhood. It was one that most of us would not believe we'd enjoy. However, if you spoke to the sisters, they would tell you that their childhood seemed normal and that they enjoyed it. They love playing chess. László even tells a story about finding Zsófia playing chess in the bathroom in the middle of the night!

This story illustrates the principle that whatever is normal in a culture will be the most desirable actions and habits for the people in that culture. Clear goes on in the chapter to discuss how this principle can help people make the habits they want to form more desirable and, therefore, easier to develop. The point I want to make is that László demonstrates the power of culture. Culture can form and shape us more than even our biological abilities. Obviously, biological abilities play an important role, and perhaps László's daughters benefited from their genes. However, their training to use their biological abilities and their deep desire to pursue greatness in chess resulted from the family culture created by their father.

If our cultures impact our lives more than anything else, then our churches must think about their cultures and seek to cultivate good, Spirit-powered cultures. The types of churches we have and the people who make up our churches primarily depend on the type of church culture we cultivate. We typically think that our church cultures are at the mercy of the personalities of the people who make them up. However, studies such as the one done by László would suggest that the personalities of the people who make up our churches are at least partially dependent on our churches' cultures. So, if we allow our church culture to be cultivated by the Holy Spirit, so will peoples' personalities.

In the end, everything about a church hinges on the church's culture, from the faithfulness of the members who make up the church to the church's ability to faithfully participate in God's story. Every person, leader and layperson alike, and everything said and done in a church contributes to how a church's culture is cultivated. I firmly believe that for us, individually and collectively, to actively participate in God's story moving into the future, we must be empowered by God's Spirit. So, for this to occur, our church cultures must also be Spirit-powered. Our leaders, members, prayers, sermons, announcements, and decisions must be governed by the Holy Spirit to develop a Spirit-powered culture that propels our churches into the future. I pray that the following survey of Paul's letters will provide a helpful starting point for your church to do just that.

2

Rome
A Culture with Vision

The Importance of Vision

For a church to cultivate a good, Spirit-powered culture, it must begin with a vision. The concept of a vision, as it applies to churches, businesses, sports teams, or any group of people, comes from the idea of seeing. A person's vision is their ability to see reality. A person can lose their vision and still see the imaginary in their mind, but a person must have vision to see reality. The better a person's vision, the better their perception of reality.

For a church to have vision, then, is for it to be able to perceive reality accurately. Generally, churches understand their vision as seeing the reality of their future, addressing questions such as: Where are we going? Where do we want to be a year from now? Five years? Ten years?

However, for a church to cultivate a culture that is genuinely Spirit-powered, its vision cannot merely be an exercise in envisioning the future; it must also envision the past and the present. Churches must ask questions such as: Where have we come from? Who are we now?

For a church to do this well—and there are plenty of ways for a church to vision poorly—the process of visioning the past, present, and future must be done with eyes open. Most churches have a vision, but the vision was created with eyes closed. The vision is not an accurate representation of reality. It is imaginary: a vision of something the church will never be able to accomplish and sometimes should not accomplish.

For example, many declining churches cast a vision that assumes they are still the thriving church they were fifty years prior, even though a church of 100 cannot vision as if they are still a church of 500. The church's people, resources, and makeup have changed, and those changes must be incorporated into the church's vision.

Another common example is a church whose community demographics have shifted. Imagine a church that has been around for 100 years. When the church was established, the community was comprised almost exclusively of white, middle to upper-class families. As time passed, the community shifted to an ethnically diverse, lower-class community, though the church remained primarily white and middle class. Such a church might be tempted to produce a vision that incorporates the needs of their current members and devise outreach programs that have worked in the past, neither of which will have much, if any, impact on their present community.

Now, by saying that a church must cast a vision with eyes open, is not to say that a church cannot or should not dream. Throughout history, true visionaries were thought by the people of their day to be seeing the imaginary when they were, in actuality, seeing a reality hidden from others. So, the church must dream. The church must recognize that through the power of the Spirit, God can do things among us that no one thought possible, but in doing so, the church must have eyes open.

Primarily, this means that the church must be honest with itself. When churches begin to create a vision, they will not always like what they see. A church is not always going to like who it was in the past or what kind of church it has become in the present. However, if a church fails to see its shortcomings, mistakes, and failures, it cannot fulfill its vision in the future.

For example, as time passes, many churches and church members become complacent. They simply go through the motions and are content with mediocrity. Church leaders can cast a perfect vision, but fulfilling the vision will be nearly impossible if the members are never moved out of their comfortable complacency. Therefore, the leaders must begin by seeing the problems currently plaguing the church and dealing with them before enacting a new vision to move the church into the future.

Two important caveats must be made at this point. First, while having a vision of the past and present that moves the church into God's future is important, this does not give license to church leaders or ministers to lead their church with an agenda. An agenda is when a church leader makes the decision to lead the church into a specific future, regardless of what the congregation or other leaders might feel about this direction. It is a self-centered leadership approach, where a leader believes they have all the answers and know what is best for the church and everyone else is wrong and blind. Such agendas only lead the church to a future where the unity God desires for his church is destroyed.

In visioning with open eyes toward the past, present, and future, church leaders must open their eyes to the makeup of their current congregation. Not every congregation is ready to make every change or pursue every possible future. For example, a church leader may believe that God desires women to have a more expansive role in the church, and they may be correct in this belief. However, the current makeup of their church may be such that they are not ready to make this change. A leader with an agenda will make the change anyway and divide the church. A Spirit-powered leader, however, will not push an agenda but seek to facilitate conversations about what God might want the church to look like and allow change to happen over time, even if that change never happens in their lifetime.

Second, churches should not cast visions as if they are a business. While the business world might provide the church with some helpful examples of healthy visions, the church is not and should not be a business. The church is the Spirit-powered people of God. Therefore, church visions should be focused on how the church can be an active participant in God's story, which is going to look drastically different than how a business or other group might operate.

For example, business visions are preoccupied with numbers. When a church casts a business vision, its focus becomes achieving goals relating to attendance, giving, and baptisms. While paying attention to metrics such as attendance, giving, and baptisms can help to give insight into a church's spiritual state, they are not always the most accurate measurements. For example, when a member who always attends suddenly stops showing up for several weeks, there might be something going on that needs a leader's attention. However, if a church with a bad culture decides to change and allow the Spirit to cultivate a new culture, there will be people who are so comfortable with the bad culture that they do not want to be a part of the new Spirit-filled culture. So, a decline in attendance may actually demonstrate a more spiritual direction than a rise in attendance.

Examples of Vision

I want to illustrate how visioning with an eye toward the past, present, and future works by returning to some examples of good culture from the last chapter.

Alabama

Consider again the Alabama football program. Alabama's winning culture must include a vision of the past. They must know from where they have come. Over the last 15 years, Alabama has consistently won games and been one of the best teams in the country. Therefore, they have become a team people love to hate. People will constantly talk bad about them in the news and on social media, and they will be booed whenever they enter an opposing team's stadium. They are going to receive everyone's best effort. Since they have been so successful, other teams will play better against them than they might against another opponent. So, because of who they have been in the past, in order to win, the Alabama players must show up to play every game, no matter their opponent.

Alabama's vision must also include the present. The coaching staff must ask: What players do we have this year? Every year, Alabama's offense and defense change based on their current roster. Things that worked with one group are not the same as what works with another group. So, to succeed, their vision must include an accurate understanding of their current team every season.

Alabama's vision must also include the future. In the future, they desire to win more championships. They have an idea of what type of team they need to be to accomplish this goal. With the knowledge of their present roster, such an understanding sheds light on the weaknesses that must be addressed to win future championships. This then influences the players they recruit. Alabama will recruit players who fit their culture and strengthen their weaknesses to achieve their vision.

Chick-fil-A

Chick-fil-A's vision includes the past. If you talk to their owners or look at their website, you will quickly realize they have never forgotten where they came from. In many ways, they still operate like the little store from which they began.

Their vision includes the present. They know who they are. According to Chick-fil-A's website, their corporate purpose is "to glorify God by being a faithful steward of all that is entrusted to us. To have a positive influence on all who come in contact with Chick-fil-A."

As a result, Chick-fil-A can have a vision for the future to live out its purpose. Most of you have probably seen the manifestations of this every time you go to Chick-fil-A, particularly in the hospitality they show their customers. A prime example is my grandmother, who, after retirement, worked several years as a Chick-fil-A greeter. Her job was greeting customers, refilling drinks, bringing sauces, and even watching a mother's kids while she went to the bathroom. Countless people benefitted from her employment, and she benefitted as well, as it gave her something to do and some purpose after retirement. The only reason Chick-fil-A would go through the trouble of hiring her and paying her salary is because of their vision. They know where they have come from, who they are, and where they are going! Great cultures have vision, and so do great churches!

Vision in Rome

In the mid-50s (55–59 CE),[1] Paul wrote a letter to the church in Rome. The church in Rome was a church that Paul did not establish and had never visited. Yet, from the letter itself, we know that he desired to travel to Rome and visit this church (Rom 1:11–13), and we know from his greetings in chapter 16 that he knew many members.

---

[1] Stanley E. Porter, *The Letter to the Romans: A Linguistic and Literary Commentary*, New Testament Monographs 37 (Sheffield: Sheffield Phoenix Press, 2015), 3; N. T. Wright, "Romans," in *Acts, Introduction to Epistolary Literature, Romans, 1 & 2 Corinthians, Galatians*, vol. IX, The New Interpreter's Bible Commentary (Nashville, TN: Abingdon Press, 2015), 350.

One of the primary occasions for the letter is tension between Jews and Gentiles (see 1:16; 9–11; 15:15–21).[2] Several years before Paul wrote Romans, all of the Jews had been kicked out of Rome, but not long before sending the letter, the Jews had been allowed to return. The church likely began as a Jewish community with Jewish leadership. They had begun incorporating Gentiles, but then they lost all of the Jews who started and had been leading the church. For several years, the church in Rome became solely a Gentile community, but recently many of the Jews had returned. You can imagine the leadership struggles this church is likely going through.[3] These issues are increased when you consider that this church is probably also struggling to figure out what role these new Gentiles play in God's story which, up to this point, had primarily included only the Jewish people.[4] So, in response, Paul writes this letter to deal with the tension by casting a vision for the Roman church.

---

[2] James D. G. Dunn, *Romans 1-8*, Word Biblical Commentary 38A (Dallas, TX: Word Books, 1988), xlv; Porter, *The Letter to the Romans: A Linguistic and Literary Commentary*, 17–18; Wright, "Romans," 327–28. There is debate as to the makeup of the Roman church and the purpose of Paul's writing. See Porter, 3-20, for a lengthy discussion of the issues. Additionally, Jew-Gentile relations are not the only occasion for Paul's writing. While I believe this to be the primary purpose, with some secondary reasons beneath, scholars debate the letter's primary purpose.

[3] Porter, *The Letter to the Romans: A Linguistic and Literary Commentary*, 9–10.

[4] Scot McKnight, "The Letter to the Romans," in *Dictionary of Paul and His Letters: A Compendium of Contemporary Biblical Scholarship*, ed. Scot McKnight (Downers Grove, IL: IVP Academic, 2023), 931–33.

Past

Paul's vision for the Roman church begins with their seeing the reality of the past. Paul begins the letter by showing that all the Christians in Rome were sinners (Rom 3:23). The Gentiles were sinners (Rom 1:18–25), but so were the Jews (Rom 2:1–5), despite the fact that the Jews did not want to admit that they were also sinners. It appears that at least some of the Jewish Christians in Rome had created an imaginary past that allowed them to pass judgment on their Gentile contemporaries. Thus Paul firmly establishes that both Jews and Gentiles are sinners (Rom 3:23) and that the wages of sin is death (Rom 6:23).

Present

Paul then moves from casting a vision of the Romans' past to casting a vision of their present. They were all sinners, but they are no longer sinners. They have been saved from their sins because of the "righteousness of God." In Romans, the righteousness of God refers to God's faithfulness to deal with sin and fulfill his covenant with Abraham (see Gn 12:1–4, 15:1–21).[5] God's righteousness has been shown through the faithfulness of Jesus[6] to God's plan (i.e., his

---

[5] This interpretation is built upon N. T. Wright's extensive work on the meaning of "the righteousness of God" in Paul. For a detailed analysis, see Wright, "Romans," 321–26.

[6] The phrase "faithfulness of Jesus" is generally translated as "faith in Jesus" (for example, see Rom 3:22 in NIV, NRSV, and ESV). Scholars debate whether the noun "Jesus" (in the genitive case) is objective ("faith in Jesus") or subjective ("faithfulness of Jesus"). Many

faithful life and faithfulness to go to the cross). Jesus's death and resurrection provide forgiveness from sin and fulfill God's promises to Abraham of a worldwide blessing and multiethnic family (i.e., the church). God's righteousness and Jesus's faithfulness benefit those who place their faith in Jesus (for an example of the connection between these themes, see Rom 3:21–26). As such, the Roman Christians, by placing their faith in Jesus, have been filled with the Holy Spirit (Rom 8:14–17), and all, both Jew and Gentile, now constitute the new Israel (Rom 9:6–8).

Future

Finally, based on their past and present, Paul concludes his letter by casting a vision for the Romans' future. Who will the Roman church be moving forward, as former sinners made righteous through the faithfulness of Jesus, who are filled and empowered by the Holy Spirit, and who now constitute the new Israel?

Paul lays out who the Romans will be in the future in Romans 12–15. This is the application portion of the letter, as is typical in Pauline Epistles. In the first two verses of chapter 12, Paul summarizes the ethical/Spirit-filled life the Romans are to live. "I appeal to you therefore, brothers and sisters, by the mercies of God, to present your bodies as a living sacrifice, holy and acceptable to God, which is your spiritual worship. Do not be conformed to this world, but be transformed by the renewing of your minds, so that you

---

scholars interpret Paul's use of the phrase as subjective, which will be the interpretation utilized in this book. See Wright, "Romans," 384.

may discern what is the will of God—what is good and acceptable and perfect."

The Roman Christians are to present themselves as "living sacrifices" to God by having their minds renewed. Rather than thinking like the rest of the world, which for Paul results in living like the world, they are to renew their minds (presumably through the power of the Spirit).[7] This is so they can "discern" or make decisions that align with God's will, so that they can determine what actions are "good and acceptable and perfect." In other words, they can fully live as the Spirit-powered people of God who are participating in God's story that has been revealed in Jesus. However, the only way for them to get to this point is to understand their past (they were sinners) and their present (they have been made righteous through Jesus and empowered by the Spirit) so that they can live as part of God's story in the future.

Our Vision

How does the modern church cast a vision in the same way Paul casts a vision for the Roman church?

Past

The process begins with accurately seeing the past. The church must cultivate a culture of evaluators. It must consistently, at minimum, at the beginning of every year, ask: Where have we succeeded over the past year? Now, here's a vital caveat. The question is not: What did we do last year

---

[7] See Paul's discussion of life in the Spirit in Rom 8:1–17.

that we liked or that we would want to do again? Too many churches and church leaders evaluate success based on their personal likes and preferences. Instead, the question is: What did we do last year that successfully moved us towards actively participating in God's worldwide story? There are plenty of things a church can do that are good and enjoyable, but if they do not fulfill the church's call to be God's image-bearers in the world, then they cannot rightly be called a success.

For example, a church may look at its food program and see that it has been able to help feed hundreds of hungry families over the past year. The leadership may then conclude that the food program was a success because they were able to show their community how much God loves them and cares for all of their needs, not just their spiritual needs.

Churches must not only evaluate successes but also failures. Where have we failed in the last year? What bad decisions did we make? Once again, the question is not: What did we not like? Just because you, your leadership team, or your congregation did not like something done or a decision made does not mean it failed at reflecting God's image. Sometimes, to accomplish a vision, you and your church must do things you don't like but are nevertheless necessary. Going back to the food program; a church's food program may take a tremendous amount of time and effort. People may not particularly like the program because of all the time it takes from them, but this does not mean the church should stop feeding people or that the program is a failure. It merely means reflecting God's image is sometimes more difficult than we would like.

Alabama football players are forced to practice five days a week but are only allowed to play once. Undoubtedly, the majority of their players do not like practice, at least not compared to playing actual games. Yet, they know they must show up every day and give 100% effort, even though they do not like it, because it is necessary for achieving their vision of future championships. The church is no different. You will have to do things you do not like to achieve what God has called you to be.

It is also essential for leaders to recognize and voice to their congregation that just because something failed does not mean that it was morally wrong or against God's will. Trial and error is a necessary process for any congregation. After a great deal of prayer, thought, and discernment, you will implement things that you firmly believe will accomplish your vision, and it will not work. That is perfectly fine. You learn, and then you move on.

Here's an example. A church decides that it needs to offer more spiritual resources to its community. So, the church starts a special summer series of lessons on relevant cultural topics to try to engage their community. They spend a summer offering these lessons, but the community never becomes involved. Ultimately, they realize that while an important part of their vision might be offering spiritual resources to their community, a series of lectures on cultural topics may be the wrong approach.

Present

A church's vision of the present begins with understanding its identity. As Paul argues throughout Romans, the church is the people of God, who place their faith in Jesus, and are empowered by the Holy Spirit. This is who the church is presently and the identity that the church must consistently live out.

Once a church has established its identity in Jesus, it must ask: Who do we have? Much like the Alabama football team every year, the church must take inventory of the talents, or spiritual gifts, available. Paul even mentions this as part of the Romans' vision (Rom 12:3–8). He says that while the church is a single, unified body, it comprises different members with different functions. Every member of the church body brings different spiritual gifts to the table for the benefit of the church.

Once a church has taken inventory of its spiritual gifts, it must ask: What does our community need and/or respond to? How can we match the spiritual gifts we have at our disposal with the things our community needs and/or responds to? What physical and/or spiritual needs are present within our church? How can we match the spiritual gifts we have at our disposal to these needs?

Perhaps the most important part of this process is accurately assessing the makeup and needs of the church's community and members. Churches are contextual entities. They exist in particular historical and geographic contexts. A church in New York does not participate in God's story in the same way as a church in Texas, nor does a church comprised of blue-collar workers participate in God's story the same way as one comprised of white-collar workers. A church must take the time to discern how God has called their particular congregation to participate in his story in their particular historical and geographic context.

This process has an inward and outward component. A church has a calling to be God's people in its community—to serve the community's needs and spread the Gospel. A church also has a calling to care for the physical and spiritual needs of the people who make up the congregation. So, the process of discerning a church's context must adequately consider both the inward and outward aspects of its calling.

The process of discerning spiritual gifts is half on church leaders. Church leaders have been tasked with discerning how to put people's spiritual gifts into practice. Leaders must lead with eyes and ears open. What do they see people are good at or drawn to? How do they see the Spirit working in the lives of their members? What gifts have members spoken about having? What are ideas and suggestions that members have made?

The other half is on members themselves. Every individual must take time to evaluate their spiritual gifts. However, most do not know how to do this on their own. So, they will need guidance. Spiritual gifts are discerned through the intersection of an outward and inward call. An inward call is how a person, individually, feels they have been gifted, where they feel the Spirit is leading them, and what they believe themselves to be good at. The outward call is how other people in the congregation, specifically spiritually mature individuals, see the Spirit at work in their lives and what they see the person is good at. When an inward and outward call intersect, you likely have a person's spiritual gifts.[8]

This can only happen through spiritual conversations. Churches should establish mentorship programs and small groups where people can engage in such conversations, especially where older, wiser members can have conversations with younger members or new converts. Leaders can put such programs in place to aid the congregation in developing its members' spiritual gifts.

Once spiritual gifts are discerned, they then must be put into practice. As mentioned above, half of this is on the leaders to discern, but the other half is on individual members. Individual members must be empowered to make suggestions about using their spiritual gifts. Leaders must cultivate a culture where people feel empowered to make suggestions to them. Perhaps this is through regular "town hall" style church meetings or a QR code to submit suggestions. Perhaps it is the leadership sharing their phone numbers and email addresses with the instructions to send them suggestions.

The leadership's response to such suggestions will make the most difference. If leaders belittle or dismiss suggestions, never follow through with implementation, or only

---

[8] Obviously, this process is not always perfect. Sometimes, a person feels both an outward and inward calling, but it turns out to be a mistake. At other times, an individual will not sense God's calling while the congregation does, or a congregation will discern God's calling before the individual. This is where trial and error comes in again. There is nothing wrong with trying something new and failing as long as the experience is used as a learning opportunity.

follow through with their personal ideas, then members will quickly become discouraged and stop making suggestions or desiring to participate. Instead, leaders must encourage and be quick to implement good suggestions. The more members can take ownership of ideas, the more engaged they will be.

The entire process must be done with a spirit of discernment. In Romans 12:1–2, Paul says we are not to conform to this world. We are not to think and act like the rest of the world, but we are to be transformed by renewing our minds. That is, we are to allow the Spirit to change the way we think. As we consider what we should do, say, or how we have been gifted, the Spirit must be our guide. As Paul says, this is so we can discern God's will, what is good and acceptable and perfect. By transforming our minds by the Spirit, we enable ourselves to answer these questions as God would.

Future

Finally, how does a church put its evaluation of the past and present into action as it moves into the future? It does so by asking the following questions: What do we repeat? What do we change? What do we stop? What do we add?

A culture of evaluators, concerned with both successes and failures, the past, and the present needs and gifts of their respective congregation and community, must put this knowledge into effect as the church moves into the future. If something was a success, repeat it. If something was a partial failure, change it. If something was a complete failure, stop it. If new needs and gifts are discovered, use them by adding something.

Everything a church does has a lifecycle. Even the best program a church has ever done will eventually become ineffective. If a church fails to evaluate and implement new ideas, they doom themselves to a vicious cycle of failed programs and a failed mission. Similarly, if a church fails to evaluate the needs of its congregation and community, it moves forward on a path where needs sit right before them but are never cared for. Neither of these options is a true reflection of God.

Here's an example from my personal ministry and life in Churches of Christ. For years, and even when I was a child, just about every church in our fellowship hosted a Vacation Bible School during the summer. Churches would be packed with kids for days, members, kids from other churches, and even kids whose families were not affiliated with any church. I imagine it could not even be quantified how many lives were impacted by the Gospel because of VBS.

However, most churches no longer get much support at VBS, both from within their congregation and from their community. Families, particularly kids, have become so busy with other activities that adding a VBS to their schedule is challenging. Yet, most churches also feel called to reach out to their community and provide biblical education. What is a church to do?

A church with no vision of the past, present, and future will continue hosting a VBS like always. They will fail to realize how the lives of their community have changed. They will fail to realize that the current format of their VBS is not achieving the desired results. So, they will fail to make any changes moving into the future. Unfortunately, many of these churches will slowly die because they failed to cast a vision.

A church with vision, however, will recognize that families are busier now than ever. That VBS was a great thing in the past, and has done tremendous good, but is no longer an adequate vessel to reach their community with the Gospel. They might begin by changing how they do VBS. Perhaps they move from a three-night event to one night. Maybe they move it from the summer to a Saturday during the school year. This might work for a while, but even these changes will eventually fail to acquire results. However, the church with a vision is not scared or dismayed by this outcome, for they know where they have come from, who they are, and where they are going. They begin brainstorming how to utilize the gifts of their congregation to do something different than a VBS. Maybe they start hosting a fifth quarter after local football games that includes a Bible study.

Regardless, through a process of trial and error, this church will eventually discern God's calling. They will find ways to reach their ever-changing community and utilize the gifts that God has blessed their congregation with. They will thrive, not necessarily numerically, but through the overflow of God's Spirit at work among them. As a result, even though it may be on a small scale, they will be faithful participants in God's worldwide story by reflecting God's image in the midst of their community.

3

Corinth
A Culture of the Cross

Another essential aspect of cultivating a good, Spirit-powered church culture is a unified purpose. If a group of people are not unified, then it is impossible for them to cultivate a good culture.

Consider again the Alabama football team. For the team to succeed, they must be unified, on the same page, and pursue the same goals. If a player is not unified with the team, then it becomes quite apparent. For example, Alabama demands every player give 100% in practice. So, you will quickly notice if a player is not giving 100% because they stand out from everyone else. If you've ever watched a football game, you've likely seen examples of a quarterback and wide receiver not being on the same page. The receiver runs one route while the quarterback throws a different route.

Consider Chick-fil-A. When you work for Chick-fil-A, you must be unified with the company's culture, goals, purpose, and values. If you are not, people notice because you don't do things in the Chick-fil-A way (perhaps you fail to say "my pleasure!"). When this happens, the store manager will call you into their office and explain that Chick-fil-A may not be the place for you.

A unified purpose is vital to the proper functioning of any group of people, and the church is no different. So, when Paul tried cultivating cultures in his churches, he consistently stressed the importance of the church's unified purpose.

The Corinthian Problem

One example is Paul's letters to the Corinthians. The church in Corinth is a church that Paul planted and one with which he has a deep, loving, and sometimes stressful relationship. This can be seen in the fact that it is one of the churches in the New Testament to which Paul writes multiple letters. In our modern Bibles, Paul's interactions with the Corinthians are divided into two letters (1 and 2 Corinthians). However, most scholars believe that 2 Corinthians was originally multiple letters that were later combined.[1] So, in

---

[1] Scholars are divided on the number of fragments in 2 Corinthians. Some hold to its continuity, others divide it into five fragments, and some doubt that every fragment is of Pauline authorship. It should be noted that we have no manuscript evidence to support such a theory. While this should not be held as a definitive reason to reject it, it does mean that the multiple letters are merely a hypothesis to explain the lack of cohesion in 2 Corinthians. For different views on the literary integrity of 2 Corinthians, see H. D. Betz, *2 Corinthians 8 and 9* (Philadelphia: Fortress Press, 1985), 90–91; D. Georgi, *The Opponents of Paul in Second Corinthians* (Philadelphia: Fortress Press, 1986), 16–18; S. J. Hafemann, "Letters to the Corinthians," in *Dictionary of Paul and His Letters*, ed. Gerald F. Hawthorne, Ralph P. Martin, and Daniel G. Reid (Downers Grove, IL: InterVarsity Press, 1993), 175–77; J. C. Hurd, *The Origin of 1 Corinthians* (London: SPCK, 1965), 235–39; and Paul J.

actuality, we have at least three letters that Paul wrote to the Corinthians, and from them, we even know that he wrote at least two more.[2]

In Paul's first letter to the Corinthians, he deals with many ethical issues in Corinth. The Corinthians are not living like followers of Jesus. Many of their issues stem from a desire for power and status, which is also causing major division within this community. They value the wisdom and rhetoric of the world (1 Cor 1:10–2:16). They are debating whether eating food offered to idols is acceptable, with some claiming to possess more or special "knowledge" (1 Cor 8:1–13). There is a division between the rich and poor while taking the Lord's Supper (1 Cor 11:17–34). They are also elevating certain spiritual gifts (1 Cor 12:1–14:40).

The problem is that the Corinthians are looking to the world to define their power and status. In the culture of the first century, the rich were typically those with power and influence.[3] It said that wisdom comes from those with eloquent speaking styles who elicit a great following.[4] As a

---

Sampley, "1 & 2 Corinthians," in *Acts, Introduction to Epistolary Literature, Romans, 1 &2 Corinthians, Galatians,* vol. IX, The New Interpreter's Bible Commentary (Nashville, TN: Abingdon Press, 2015), 868–72.

[2] See 1 Cor 5:9–12 and 2 Cor 2:9, 7:8–12. Hafemann, "Letters to the Corinthians," 175–77; Sampley, "1 & 2 Corinthians," 669 and 870.

[3] Duane F. Watson, "Roman Social Classes," in *Dictionary of New Testament Background: A Compendium of Biblical Scholarship,* ed. Stanley E. Porter and Craig A. Evans (Downers Grove, IL: InterVarsity Press, 2000), 999.

[4] Hafemann, "Letters to the Corinthians," 165.

result, the Corinthians elevate the rich around the Lord's Table. They elevate the spiritual gifts that resemble worldly wisdom (e.g., speaking in tongues and prophecy). They even elevate people based on who baptized them, likely because of their rhetorical skills (1 Cor 1:12).[5]

The Corinthians have allowed what takes place outside the church, in their Greco-Roman culture, to come inside and become a part of their church culture. As a result, Paul fears that they risk destroying everything God has built.

Modern Wisdom

Unfortunately, the contemporary church also has a bad habit of allowing the things that take place outside the church, in our twenty-first-century American culture, to creep inside the church and become a part of our church culture. When the church does so, it risks worshipping and following something other than God. Remember that culture is powerful. The people in our churches are not only being influenced by our church culture but also by the American culture they live in. The church can and should celebrate the good things present in all cultures while maintaining that the church is not to look like those other cultures. As a group that is in the world but not of the world, the church's culture should be unique.

Therefore, for the church to have a Spirit-powered, Christ-centered culture it must have a unified purpose. Everyone in the church must be on the same page. They must be pursuing the same goals. They must all desire to cultivate

---

[5] Hafemann.

the same culture. They cannot be like the wide receiver running one route while the quarterback throws a different route.

So, churches, and the individuals who make up those churches, must ask themselves: Who do you serve? Who do you follow? Who do you listen to? Where do you find your wisdom?

Yourself

Is it yourself? Do you simply do whatever you want? Do you determine what is right and wrong and what is wise based on your opinion?

Depending on who you ask, we live in either a post-modern or post-post-modern world. Regardless, post-modernism is not actually a thing. That is, post-modernism does not assert or believe in anything. Rather, post-modernism is simply a rejection of modernism. It rejects modernism's appeal to objectivity. Post-modernism says that no one and nothing is truly objective; everyone has ulterior motives and biases.

This assertion by post-modern thought is undoubtedly true. No one can be totally objective. The way we think about things is determined by our experiences, upbringing, and education. I do believe we should strive to be fair in our evaluations. That is, we should try to take in all the facts and recognize our intellectual shortcomings and biases. However, while this process can be fair, it cannot be objective. We will never be able to totally identify our intellectual shortcomings and biases, not to mention that those shortcomings and biases will determine what we gather as the evidence for our biases.

The problem with post-modernism is not that it asserts our inability to be objective. The problem is that it does not continue developing this concept to suggest ways that people, despite their intellectual shortcomings, biases, and ulterior motives can come to know anything. It rejects objectivity but gives nothing to fill its place.

The result is a world that has fallen into complete subjectivity. Everything is subjective truth; nothing is objective truth. There is your truth and my truth. There are plenty of truths that are subjective. To say that *Friends* is the best TV show is a subjective truth. However, there are other truths that are objective: that the sky is blue, or that God is the creator of the universe.

Since our world defines truth subjectively, the individual becomes the ultimate assessor of truth. Something is only true if I want it to be true or if it is true for me. Therefore, what is right and wrong, good and evil, better and best is not determined by any source outside of the individual. In the end, the result is a world where everyone follows themselves.

If you don't believe this is a prominent belief in the church, then you haven't talked to many people. We are going to disagree about the interpretation and application of biblical passages, and that is perfectly fine. However, it disturbs me to see the number of people, when you ask them a question on which the Bible has a lot to say on the subject, respond with, "Well, I think …" For those who follow Jesus, our initial response should always be, "Well, God says …"

We don't always have to agree on what we think God is saying, but we should always root our beliefs in our faith.

News, Social Media, Politics

What about the news? Social media? A particular political figure? As mentioned, in Paul's day people connected wisdom with a person's speaking ability. The better speaker someone was, and the more followers they had, the more people believed that their speaking contained wisdom. An honest look at our contemporary society, and even within our churches, will show that we are no different.

We like a news anchor not so much because what they say makes any sense, but because they look good, sound good, and keep us in our comfort zone. We take advice from people on social media because they, too, look good, sound good, and have a large following. We vote for a political figure because they look good, sound good, represent the "right" political party, and advocate for policies that keep us in charge, powerful, and maintain our status. We are no different than the Corinthians in Paul's day.

Our society has become very bad at evaluating the sources from which we get our information and wisdom and, ultimately, the sources that influence our opinions, thoughts, and decisions. This is not a book on the American education system, but a comment needs to be made. I know many good teachers who give everything they have to better their students. However, in many ways, they are limited by being forced to teach solely for grades on a standardized test. Teacher performance, pay, and school grant money are connected to these tests. As a result, most students are taught information recall, not how to evaluate and utilize this information. In a world of the internet, Google, and artificial intelligence, we have more information at our fingertips than we could ever utilize, except we don't know what to do with it, what to think about it, or how to evaluate where this information is coming from.

Most churches recognize the major problems in our world and feel called by God to participate in God's redemption of these evils. However, most members of church congregations look for their solutions to these problems, not in God, Scripture, or their local church, but on TikTok, Fox News, or the Democratic Party. How should we respond to poverty? "Well, this girl on TikTok says …" How should we respond to gun violence? "Well, my Fox News anchor says …" How should we respond to racism? "Well, the Democratic party says …" The problem is that most of the people sitting in your church pews know the problems that exist but look for wise solutions in the wrong place.

Favorite Preacher

Many Christians who do look for wisdom in their faith find it in their favorite preacher or Christian author. It is beneficial to listen and read different people with different perspectives. Different speakers and authors have different gifts that can benefit a person's spiritual journey. One preacher may be gifted in explaining the meaning of a text, while another is gifted in giving illustrations that allow the text to come to life. One author may emphasize the Old Testament connection in a New Testament passage, while another might be knowledgeable about the Greco-Roman context of the passage.

However, it must be remembered that another person's context is not your context. Someone may be teaching perfect theology and applying it soundly to their context, but that application does not necessarily work in another context. Too often, churches want to do something because they see it working in another church, but that does not mean it will work in their church and their context. Nor does it mean that God has called them to be exactly like that other church. There are things God might be trying to do through them that they are uniquely qualified to accomplish, but which your church is not.

It seems that every small church wants to be like the big church down the road. They need the same social media presence. They need to do the big, expensive events. They need the coffee bar and children's area. Nothing is wrong with any of these things, but it is not necessarily the type of church that God calls the small church to be. Sometimes, God wants a small church to be small because it provides things to the community that the big church cannot. For example, many small churches provide a family-style approach to church that a larger church cannot emulate. Conversely, the large church has resources to do things the small church cannot. Just as every individual fills a unique role in the church, every church fills a unique role in God's mission to the world.

Traditions

Sometimes, our traditions take center stage for where we find our wisdom. This is how we've always done it or what we've always believed, so it must be the source of wisdom. Traditions are essential; they give meaning to our practices. However, we must be critical of our traditions and not become too comfortable with them. Just because we have always done and believed something does not mean it is (or is not) correct or best. This is why we must critically evaluate all our traditions and is also why our church visions must include the past, present, and future.

Relating to traditions, here is a suggestion if your church is struggling. If you feel like your church cannot get ahead and is constantly dealing with one issue after another, try placing all your traditions on the chopping block. Everything you do is up for debate and has the opportunity to be changed, with the exceptions of your core theological convictions (e.g., following Jesus is not up for debate). The key question to ask is what type of church do you want to build for the future and pursue traditions that are in line with this vision. By engaging in such an exercise, you are not deciding to change anything. What you are doing is opening up yourself to evaluating your long-held traditions and asking yourself what type of church you want to be moving into the future.

Experiences

For others, experiences are the most important source of true wisdom. While a great deal of wisdom can be gleaned from personal experience, it cannot necessarily be generalized. This is why studies in the social sciences are conducted by comparing the personal experiences of hundreds or thousands of people to find common trends that can then be generalized to the larger population.

Here are some examples of how this works. If personal experience can automatically be generalized, then a skydiver whose parachute never opened and survived his fall could say, "Everyone should stop using a parachute when they skydive because I didn't use one and survived. So, you will, too!" Two spouses who physically abuse one another and yet were married for 60 years could say, "Every couple should abuse each other like we did because we had a long marriage!" The problem is that these happened on a small, isolated scale, but we know they don't happen on a larger, more generalized scale. When we look at all skydivers, we see that people generally don't survive when their parachutes don't open. When we look at all marriages, we see that, generally, abusive marriages do not last. Since experience cannot easily be generalized, if your experiences are your ultimate guide, you will eventually find yourself in some deep trouble because you'll realize your experience does not consistently work or work for everyone.

Here's the point: if the members of a church serve, follow, or listen to anything or anybody other than Jesus, then that church will be divided because everyone will be following something or someone different. One person may be following Jesus, but another their desires, another their favorite news anchor, another their favorite social media personality, another their favorite political figure, another their favorite preacher, another their traditions, and another their personal experiences. In the end, the church is fragmented.

The Corinthian Culture of the Cross

For this reason, when Paul addresses these issues in Corinth, his solution is quite simple: the Corinthians need to cultivate a culture of the cross.

Set Apart

Paul begins 1 Corinthians by saying that the Corinthians are "sanctified" and "called to be saints" (1 Cor 1:2). Both terms are derived from the Greek root word "holy." Holiness means to be set apart. In a religious context, it means that something is set apart for God. For example, in the Old Testament, the temple was holy, containing the holy place and the holy of holies. There was nothing special about the temple in and of itself. It was just a building. What made the temple special is that this building was set apart as the dwelling place of God and where sacrifices were made on behalf of Israel.

Similarly, Paul says that the Corinthians have been set apart for service to God. They are not to live like the rest of the world but as people set apart from the world. As Paul will go on to say, they are specifically not to accept their worldly culture wholesale.

Purpose

Paul goes on in the first chapter to say that all the Corinthians are to "be in agreement" and there are to be "no divisions among you," but they are to be "united in the same mind and the same purpose" (1 Cor 1:10). As people set apart for God, they must have the same purpose, goal, and destination.

Follow the One Crucified

In verses 11–17, Paul continues to identify their unified purpose. He talks about how the Corinthians are divided based on who baptized them. One says, "I belong to Paul," and another, "I belong to Apollos," and yet another, "I belong to Cephas." Paul's response is to ask three questions: "Has Christ been divided? Was Paul crucified for you? Or were you baptized in the name of Paul?" (v. 13). Paul is asking why the Corinthians would follow someone who was not crucified for them and why they would declare their allegiance to Jesus in their baptism and not follow him. The Corinthians' purpose should be to follow Jesus, who died for them and whose death, burial, and resurrection they reenacted in their baptism (see Rom 6:1–11).

New Kingdom

In the next section (1 Cor 1:18–25), Paul speaks of the surpassing greatness of God's wisdom. He states that even God's foolishness is wiser than the wisest person on earth. For ages, the world has operated based on its definition of power, status, and wisdom—the people with money rule, and wisdom is based on a person's rhetorical skills and education, but God has changed this arrangement. God has established a new kingdom with new rules and a new ruler. This kingdom was established not through force, war, or worldly wisdom, but through death on a cross. The cross of

Christ established a new kingdom. Therefore, power, status, and wisdom have now, and forever, been redefined by a cross.

It's important to realize how countercultural this idea is. The cross was a means of public torture for the enemies of Rome. It was a symbol of defeat and weakness, not of a king's victory. However, through the humiliation of the cross, Jesus conquered the powers of evil and established an everlasting kingdom. Therefore, in this kingdom, power, status, and wisdom are defined by the weakened image of a cross.

God Works Through Weakness

In this new kingdom, defined by a cross, God does not necessarily work through the rich and powerful, though he can do so: but at times, and Paul might even have in mind most of the time, God works through the weak, lowly, and despised. Paul emphasizes something similar in 2 Corinthians. In that letter, Paul primarily deals with false apostles who have begun influencing the church and trying to steer the Corinthians away from Paul. As a result, he is forced to defend his apostleship. At one point, Paul counters a claim by the false apostles that they receive their authority from visions by recounting his vision. Paul, in essence, says, "If you want to talk about visions, I have a vision that can outdo anything you claim to have experienced."

However, Paul concludes by saying that visions of grandeur don't define him. "So, I will boast all the more gladly of my weaknesses so that the power of Christ may dwell in me. Therefore I am content with weaknesses, insults, hardship, persecutions, and calamities for the sake of Christ; for whenever I am weak, then I am strong" (2 Cor 12:9b–10).

Power in God's kingdom is defined by a cross. Through the weakness of the cross, Jesus conquered the powers of evil, establishing the kingdom of God. Therefore, true power is made perfect in weakness, for our power does not come from ourselves but from the power of God through the Holy Spirit.

Our Culture of the Cross

As citizens of the kingdom of God, Christians play by new rules. Power, greatness, and wisdom were forever redefined on that day, two thousand years ago, when the Son of God went to a cross. True wisdom and power are now seen through the lens of the cross. How can churches cultivate a culture of the cross?

Live as Saints

First, they live as saints. The church is in the world but not of the world. As people in the world, the church must engage with the world. It cannot hide from the world in the comfort of homes and church buildings. Jesus says we are to be a light to the world (Mt 5:14–16) and are to make disciples of all nations (Mt 28:18–20). We must meet people where they are: in hospitals, shelters, next door, or on Tik-Tok. We must engage our world's questions, concerns, and advancements, allowing God to speak into them rather than letting the world do all the talking.

However, while we must live in the world, we can never forget that we are not of the world. We do not accept everything in the world wholesale. We must utilize the wisdom of God through his Spirit, Scripture, and the church to evaluate the things of the world.

So, churches and preachers must address the topics of the day. When there is a school shooting or a presidential election, churches cannot hide from these conversations. If the church hides, then the world (i.e., the news or social media) will be where our members find their wisdom. Instead, Christians should be able to walk through the doors of their church and hear how God addresses the real issues they are thinking about and dealing with Monday through Saturday.

Churches must seek after people where they are. Many of the people who need God most are in hospitals alone, recovering from surgery. They are in shelters trying to figure out where they are going to get their next meal. They are searching for human connections on TikTok, YouTube, and Instagram.[38] Does your church have a presence in these places, or have you retreated to the comfort of your church building, waiting for people to come find you?

The church's call to reach the world is built on its rejection of the world's post-modern claim to subjectivity. The church must balance the reality that no person can be completely objective with the equally true reality that objective truth is found in the person of Jesus Christ. The church's proclamation as a community of people in the world but not of the world is that we possess a truth that the world does not have access to: the truth of God revealed in Jesus Christ.

Therefore, our pursuit of truth must begin with Jesus, who is "the way, the truth, and the life" (Jn 14:6), with the primary witness to Jesus being Scripture. The truth found in Jesus is seen most clearly in the cross. In the cross, Paul says that we have been given

> the knowledge of the glory of God in the face of Jesus Christ. But we have this treasure in clay jars, so that it may be made clear that this extraordinary power belongs to God and does not come from us. We are afflicted in every way, but not crushed; perplexed, but not driven to despair; persecuted, but not forsaken; struck down, but not destroyed; always carrying in the body the death of Jesus, so that the life of Jesus may also be made visible in our bodies. For while we live, we are always being given up to death for Jesus' sake, so that the life of Jesus may be made visible in our mortal flesh. (2 Cor 4:6c–11)

The problem, as post-modernism noticed, is that human beings are incapable of being purely objective when seeking to understand truth. As we look at the truth in Jesus, there will always be a cloudy haze between us and truth, made up of our presuppositions and biases. So, how do we go about uncovering the truth found in Jesus?

The answer is the Holy Spirit. The Spirit guides us into all truth (Jn 16:13), but the Spirit works most powerfully in a community of believers. Each Christian possesses the Holy Spirit, but when a community of Spirit-empowered people comes together, it creates a whole new kind of spiritual temple. Primarily, the church provides a community where Spirit-indwelt people can engage in conversation and debate in their effort to uncover the truth found in Jesus. Through the different personalities, experiences, and spiritual gifts of the church, the Spirit is able to guide us to all truth.

Purpose

Second, a church must be unified in purpose. Our ultimate purpose is to be transformed into the image of Jesus (Rom 8:29). However, the way this looks is different for different groups of people in different contexts. Therefore, I believe it is vital for churches to craft a vision or mission statement to help guide the way a contextualized congregation thinks, what it does, and the decisions that it makes. When a difficult decision arises, the church can return to its vision and ask what decision holds to its purpose.[6]

Follow the One Crucified

Third, a church must follow the one who died on a cross for them, the one whose death was reenacted in their baptism. A church and its members can find themselves following all sorts of things and people who did not die for them. Think for a moment about some of the silly things people can get bent out of shape about: congregations splitting over the color of the carpet, the number of new versus old hymns, or the person leading at the front. We can get so mad because we don't get our way, or our favorite tradition

---

[6] See Appendix II, "How to Use Social Media."

was changed, or someone did not take our experience into account, things that Jesus never died for.

Let's get one thing straight: Jesus didn't die for your opinion. He didn't die for your tradition. He didn't die for your experiences. Jesus died to save you from the powers of sin and evil in the world. So, let's ensure that the battles we choose to fight are on hills for which Jesus died. A church should be going to battle against the powers of sin and evil in the world, not the color of the carpet or the hymns sung in worship.

This is not to say that opinions, traditions, or experiences are unimportant. In 1 Corinthians 8, Paul deals with the different opinions in Corinth over eating meat sacrificed to idols. His point is to demonstrate the importance of being considerate of a brother or sister's conscience. Discussing opinions, having traditions, and utilizing experiences are important for a healthy church culture. The problem is when the church's future hinges on accepting a particular opinion, tradition, or experience rather than on the cross of Christ.

Let's also remember that your favorite news anchor, social media influencer, or political leader would not go to a cross for you. You might think they care about you, but chances are they couldn't care less, and even if they do, they will not die for you. You know who did die for you? Jesus!

Let's follow the man crucified for us and fight the battles for which he died! This means that church leaders cannot allow battles to be fought over things for which Jesus did not die. Too often, church leaders desire to please everyone, which is ultimately impossible. Someone is always going to be unhappy. The goal of a church and church leaders is not to please every congregation member but to please God by being active participants in God's worldwide story.

So don't waste your time figuring out how to change something that is working to please one unhappy person. Develop the courage to stand by your decisions to follow the Spirit's guidance, even when most people don't like them, and be humble enough to admit fault when you make the wrong decision. Display love for people by directing them back to the cross when they become overly concerned with unimportant matters.

Perhaps the best way to keep people focused on the cross is to keep them busy in the way of the cross. When people are serving, teaching, and showing Jesus in their community, they usually don't have time to worry about the carpet or song choices. Find ways to get people involved, and make yourself an example of servant leadership, and many of the peripheral problems will disappear.

A New Kingdom

The church is part of a kingdom that is not of this world, the kingdom of God. Current and future political leaders, social media influencers, prominent and influential companies, and the rich and famous may look like they are in control, but in reality, God has taken complete control. So why build a church to look like them?

Churches cannot cultivate consumer cultures, enabling our members to think we will operate like their favorite business. The church is not Burger King; you can't always "have it your way." Just because a member threatens to pull their contribution does not mean a church changes what it believes God has called the church to accomplish.

Churches cannot enable their members to think that their money, possessions, influence, or followers actually matter or substantially impact their happiness and satisfaction. True joy only comes from the presence of God in our lives. The best way to do this is through preaching and teaching on the topics going on in the world and about which our congregation members are thinking about and concerned.

Churches must teach their congregants to think critically and not believe everything they hear. Someone will always say that the sky is falling, but a presidential candidate is not the one who holds up the sky. That is God's job.

God Works Through Weakness

Finally, our churches must believe that God works through weakness. God is seen and experienced, not through church cultures built on an individual's strengths and abilities, but on the power of God through the indwelling of the Holy Spirit. Spirit-powered, Christ-centered church cultures rely on God to do the heavy lifting. They pursue things that are impossible based on their collective strength, realizing that it is incredibly possible with God's power. This is so that, when all is said and done, no one can look at them and claim that they have accomplished anything but are forced to give glory to God.

A church finds its power not in a good business strategy, a preacher with great speaking skills, the right program, or the right building design. The church finds its power in God through the indwelling of the Holy Spirit. As your church considers developing a vision for the future, try pursuing things that you know are impossible if God doesn't show up. Otherwise, you are putting your future in your hands rather than God's. By pursuing impossible things, we allow God to do the impossible.

Interlude

The Cross and the Table

One key place where a culture of the cross is experienced is at the Lord's Table during the church's partaking of the Lord's Supper. As previously discussed, Paul wrote 1 Corinthians to deal with problems within the Corinthian community. One of the primary issues is the Corinthians' desire for power and status, which they defined based upon a worldly standard rather than the cross. One place this issue is seen is when the Corinthians gather to take the Lord's Supper.

In 1 Corinthians 11:17–22, Paul addresses some division between rich and poor around the Lord's Table. 1 Corinthians 11 is our earliest account of the Lord's Supper, predating Mark's account by about fifteen years. The earliest practice of the Lord's Supper, as evidenced by 1 Corinthians 11, was part of a common meal, likely rooted in the fact that Jesus instituted the Lord's Supper as part of the Passover meal. However, when the Corinthians gather for this meal, the rich get full and drunk while the poor are left hungry.

Paul deals with this division by, once again, cultivating a culture of the cross. In 11:23–26, Paul recounts the Lord's Supper tradition he received from Jesus. Paul's account reads similarly to the accounts in Matthew, Mark, and Luke, but with three notable differences. First, after breaking and blessing the bread, Paul has Jesus saying, "This is my body that is for you." Only Paul and Luke include the phrase "for you." For Paul, Jesus's giving up of his body on the cross is an act for Jesus's followers. It is for their benefit, salvation, and transformation.

Following this statement, Paul has Jesus saying, "Do this in remembrance of me." Once again, only Paul and Luke include the statement of Jesus that his followers are to continue taking of the bread to remember him. Jesus then takes the cup and says, "This cup is the new covenant in my blood. Do this, as often as you drink it, in remembrance of me." Once again, Jesus says his followers are to continue taking the cup to remember him, and only Paul includes this second reference to remembrance. Remembrance for Jews such as Paul, Luke,[1] Jesus, the disciples, and the earliest followers of Jesus was an important virtue. In Judaism, to remember the past is to bring the past into the present in a way that impacts the present.

For example, in Deuteronomy 26:5–11, Moses begins recounting the story of Abraham and his descendants who ended up in Egypt. Moses begins by speaking in the third person about a "wandering Aramean," "my ancestor," and "he." These are events that happened in the past to other people. Then, Moses switches to the first person, using words such as "us," "we," "our," "I," and "me." For Moses and Israel to remember the story of Abraham is to make Abraham's past story Israel's present story. Since Israel is living as a part of a story that goes back to God's activity with

---

[1] There is debate as to whether the author of Luke-Acts was a Hellenistic Jew or a Gentile believer.

Abraham, there are present implications for Israel. They must "bring the first fruits of the ground" to their Lord.

When Paul says that the Corinthians are to remember Jesus's body and blood as they take the Lord's Supper, he is saying that they are to remember Jesus's story—his birth, life, death, resurrection, ascension, and eventual return to usher in the new creation. However, this story is not merely a story of the past or future; it is a story with present implications. The Corinthians are to take this past story and make it their present story. The Corinthians are to live as active participants in Jesus's story, which results in a particular life now.

This is why Paul says that when they take the Lord's Supper, they proclaim "the Lord's death until he comes." When the Corinthians take the Lord's Supper, remembering Jesus's story and making Jesus's story their story, the result is that they proclaim Jesus's story to the world because it has become their story.

Paul then moves on in verses 27–34 to apply these principles to the division in Corinth. He says that the Corinthians must ensure they are not taking the Lord's Supper in an "unworthy manner." By this, Paul does not mean that they must have a perfect relationship with Jesus, have their mind right, or that non-believers and children cannot take the Lord's Supper.[2] Rather, Paul is referring to the problem

---

[2] Allowing non-believers, children, and those with low-functioning disabilities to take the Lord's Supper is referred to as open communion. Open communion is a controversial issue. Regardless of where you stand, this is not what Paul addresses in this passage.

he mentioned in verses 17–22; that the Corinthians are divided between rich and poor around the table.

So, the Corinthians are to "examine themselves." They are to think about and evaluate their life, thoughts, words, and actions relating to the current division. This is because "all who eat and drink without discerning the body, eat and drink judgment against themselves." The NIV reads, "without discerning the body of Christ." Some manuscripts of 1 Corinthians have the phrase "of Christ," but the best and earliest manuscripts omit the phrase. So, Paul's original statement was "without discerning the body." The question is, what body are the Corinthians to discern?

Throughout 1 Corinthians, Paul uses the word body (gk. σῶμα, *soma*) to refer to three different bodies: Jesus's physical body, the body of Christ in the church, and believers' physical bodies. In this verse, Paul does not specify to which body he refers. Therefore, we must allow the context to determine Paul's referent.

In chapter 11, Paul uses the word *body* three times. First, in verse 24, Jesus is instituting the Lord's Supper and says, "This is my *body* that is given for you." Second, in verse 27, Paul says that the one who takes the Supper in an unworthy manner "will be answerable for the *body* and blood of the Lord." Finally, in verse 29, Paul says that the Corinthians are to discern the body. So, the immediate context would suggest that Paul is referring to Jesus's physical body as seen in the bread of the Lord's Supper.

However, to fully understand Paul's words, we must go back to what he said earlier in the letter. In 10:16–17, he states that "The cup of blessing that we bless, is it not a sharing in the blood of Christ? The bread that we break, is it not a sharing in the *body* of Christ? Because there is one bread, we who are many are one *body*, for we all partake of the one bread." Paul says that when the Corinthians take of the bread in the Lord's Supper, they are taking of the body of Christ. However, weirdly, they also partake in the church because the church is also the body of Christ. While Christ's body in the Lord's Supper is unique from the church, it is also the same as the church, both being the body of Christ.

What makes up the body of Christ in the church are the individual bodies of believers, which Paul speaks about when addressing sexual immorality in 6:20. "For you were bought with a price; therefore glorify God in your *body*." The death of Jesus's physical body, which is remembered in the bread and cup of the Lord's Supper, purchased the individual bodies of believers from sin and death. Therefore, believers are to glorify God in how they use our bodies.

So, with the entire context of 1 Corinthians in view, the following interpretation of Paul's words in 1 Corinthians 11:27–29 seems to fit. The Corinthians are divided between rich and poor around the Lord's Table. However, when they take the Lord's Supper, remembering Jesus's story, they make Jesus's story their own story. They live as part of the story of Jesus, who gave up his body and shed his blood on the cross for them. To live as part of this story, that is, to live like Jesus, means that they, too, must give of themselves for others. If the Corinthians are willing to give of themselves for others, then there is no way they could be divided around the Lord's Table.

Therefore, what the Corinthians need to do as they take the Lord's Supper is discern Jesus's body. They first must remember Jesus's story, when Jesus went to a cross to give of his body for them, which is now their story. Second, they must remember that they are not only part of this story, but they are also Jesus's body, the church. Therefore, as Jesus's body, they must cultivate a culture of the cross that looks like Jesus's body, which is a body that is unified, not divided. Finally, they need to look at their individual bodies, which comprise Jesus's body, the church. They must ask, "How is my body contributing to the division in Christ's body as I partake of Christ's body in the Lord's Supper?" So for the Corinthians to eat the Lord's Supper in an unworthy manner is for them to partake of Christ's body in the bread while allowing their personal bodies to divide the body of Christ, the church.

When Paul's words are taken to heart, I believe they illustrates that the primary place that a culture of the cross is cultivated in our churches is around the Lord's Table as we take the Lord's Supper. When the church assembles to take the Lord's Supper, we remember the story of Jesus. Not merely Jesus's death but also his birth, life, resurrection, ascension, and even his return and ushering in the new creation. This entire story is what Paul has in mind every time he uses the word "cross." For Paul, the term cross is a catchall word or shorthand for Jesus's entire story.

We remember that the cross shows us a Lord who gave of himself for others, modeled servant leadership, and did not come to be served but to serve. To remember Jesus's story is to make Jesus's story our own story. We live in our bodies the way Jesus lived in his. We live out a culture of the cross.

Second, as we partake of Jesus's body in the bread of the Lord's Supper, we remember that we are a part of this body. You and I fill unique and essential roles in Christ's body. The body of Christ cannot function without you and the gifts the Holy Spirit has given you. Additionally, we must constantly ask whether our church body actually looks like Christ's body. Is our church operating in a way that proclaims the story of Jesus to the world? Is our church divided? How does our church treat the poor and outcast? Once again, is our church cultivating a culture of the cross?

I want to make a brief side comment about the church's treatment of the poor and outcast, though an entire book should be written on the subject. Following a man who gave his life to save others illustrates the church's responsibility to give of itself for others, particularly those in need. The Gospel with the greatest emphasis on the Lord's Supper is the Gospel of Luke, which also happens to be the Gospel that illustrates Jesus's care for the poor and outcast. The church has the same responsibility. How does your church treat the poor, widows, orphans, minorities, refugees, and illegal immigrants?

This is one reason I support open communion (i.e., communion opened to the unbaptized), though I believe there is a scriptural precedence. By opening communion to those outside of our body, the church models and cultivates a culture of the cross that is open to and cares for outsiders. Once again, I believe that the best place to model and cultivate such a culture is when the church gathers around the table.

Finally, each of us must also examine our individual bodies. Does my body look like Christ's body? Is my body contributing to division within Christ's body? Is my body preventing my church body from looking like Jesus? Am I using my body to benefit Christ's body? Is my body cultivating a culture of the cross?

So churches must make their practice of the Lord's Supper a moment where a culture of the cross is cultivated. When was the last time you taught or preached about the meaning and purpose of the Lord's Supper? What is said before partaking of the Supper? The words that prepare people for partaking of the Lord's Supper are vital to creating an atmosphere where the Supper is allowed to cultivate a culture of the cross. Each time we gather around the table, people must be reminded that this is a moment when Jesus is present with us, and we place ourselves into Jesus's story.

The way we take the Lord's Supper can also either help or hurt our ability to allow the Supper to cultivate a culture of the cross. If we make the Supper a time to be quiet, solemn, and to think only of Jesus's death, then we are missing the fullness of the Supper. The Lord's Supper is not a funeral for a dead man but a celebration for a man who rose from the dead. The Supper is not merely a time to consider the implications of the cross but the cruciform life Jesus lived in every moment.

Nor is the Lord's Supper a moment only for the individual and their relationship with Jesus. The Lord's Supper is a communal experience. We call it communion because we commune not just with Jesus but also with one other. It is a moment for the church collectively to consider its relationship with its membership and community. It is a time for the entire congregation to analyze their culture and whether or not it reflects the cross.

The primary problem with making the Lord's Supper a communal experience is the design of our modern church auditoriums. Church auditoriums are designed like lecture halls, focusing on the elevated platform where speaking, preaching, and worship performances occur. They are not designed like tables where the church can gather together as a community of believers. This means we must be intentional about how our worship services, particularly the Lord's Supper, are carried out. How can we partake in a way that emphasizes communion with one another?

There is no easy or simple answer to this problem. However, here are a couple of possible solutions: Sing a song during the Lord's Supper, allowing the entire church to raise their voices to God together. Have your congregation gather in small groups to partake. Perhaps you could even set up small tables around your auditorium to facilitate the feeling of a table gathering. If your congregation is small enough, you could have everyone stand up and gather in a circle while you partake.

I don't think, generally speaking, that there is a right or wrong way for a congregation to take the Lord's Supper. I do believe, however, that there are better and worse ways. I think some ways can facilitate the communal aspect of the Supper and help to cultivate a culture of the cross and ways that emphasize other, and even contradictory, ideas.

Therefore, it is vital for churches and church leaders to spend time thinking, discussing, and discerning the Spirit's guidance in how they take the Lord's Supper. What does their structure teach their congregation about their values and beliefs? How does their structure help or hurt their desire to cultivate a culture of the cross?

4

Galatia
A Culture of Unity

One of the most important aspects of cultivating good, Spirit-powered church cultures is unity. Throughout the Old and New Testaments, one can pick up on the crucial role that unity plays among the people of God.[1] God has called his people (Israel and the church) into existence to reflect his image to the world. In order for God's people to fulfill such a task, they must be unified.

There are two different types of unity. First, there is unity of purpose, which we discussed in the previous chapter. Churches must be unified in pursuing the one crucified for them. There is also a unity of people. A group of people can be unified in purpose, but if they are not unified as people (i.e., if they don't like or want to be around each other), then their unified purpose is useless.

For example, the individual players on a sports team can all desire to win a championship, but if they don't like or want to be around each other, then they probably won't be able to succeed. In my experience as a college basketball

---

[1] Ps 133:1; Zech 14:9; Jn 17:20–21; Eph 4:3.

player, the better teammates get along off the court, the better they play on it.

This principle is why companies encourage their employees to engage in team-building exercises. Companies know that while employees might all desire the same purpose (i.e., the leadership has done an excellent job of casting a vision for the company), there must be team chemistry to achieve that purpose. So they do team building exercises, perhaps the popular "trust fall," to better unite the people pursuing these goals.

The Galatian Situation

We see an emphasis on personal unity in Paul's letter to the Galatians. Galatians is one of the first, and some scholars argue it is the first,[2] letter of Paul in the New Testament. The issue in Galatia is their understanding of the Jewish law and how it relates to those in Christ, causing division within the Galatian community.

Specifically, Jewish false teachers have entered the Galatian community and are teaching that a Gentile must be circumcised before becoming a follower of Jesus. In other words, they are teaching that a Gentile must become a Jew

---

[2] Charles B. Cousar, *Galatians*, Interpretation: A Bible Commentary for Preaching and Teaching (Louisville, KY: Westminster John Knox Press, 2012), 6–7; Richard N. Longenecker, *Galatians*, Word Biblical Commentary 41 (Dallas, TX: Word Books, 1990), lxxii–lxxxviii; Richard B. Hays, "Galatians," in *Acts, Introduction to Epistolary Literature, Romans, 1 & 2 Corinthians, Galatians*, vol. IX, The New Interpreter's Bible Commentary (Nashville, TN: Abingdon Press, 2015), 1027–29.

before entering the Christian community. They believe that access to God is through the Jewish nation and the Jewish law. In essence, the Jewish false teachers are saying, "You have to become like us to have access to God."

The false teachers do not necessarily desire division among the Christians in Galatia. On the contrary, they likely desire to unite the Galatians, just under their specific qualifications. However, their desire for unity is a unity without diversity. They do not seem to believe that there can be much diversity between Jews and Gentiles in the church but that everyone must become like a Jew, look like a Jew, and live like a Jew.

The Church's Temptation

Modern Christians and churches have the same temptation as the false teachers in Galatia. Too often, Christianity is approached with the mindset, "You have to become like us to have access to God." While most Christians would never say these words or believe they would ever support such a stance, too often, the church's actions reflect this very sentiment. When a church makes non-essential issues essential to salvation, to be in good standing with God, or for membership in the church they are telling people that they must become and look like them to have access to God.

Read through Galatians and notice that Paul has no problem with people following the Jewish law or being circumcised. On the contrary, Paul believes both are good because he does both himself. However, Paul draws the line at making other people do the same because though they may be good and even enhance a person's relationship with God, he knows that one's relationship with God is not dependent on them. So, when we draw lines of fellowship based on non-essential issues, no matter how good our stance may be or how much it might enhance a person's relationship with God, we fail to cultivate the type of church culture of which Paul would approve.

The question then becomes, what is considered an essential versus non-essential issue? Where should a church draw lines of fellowship? Every church that draws fellowship lines does so because they believe the line to be an essential, biblical issue. So, how do we distinguish?

This is a challenging and multifaceted issue that I believe can only be answered through spending a great deal of time in discernment, meditation, and prayer through the power of the Holy Spirit. Church leaders and ministers must spend a great deal of time in prayer and with the Spirit before deciding where official church lines will be drawn. I would encourage all churches to take the time to go through a period of discernment regarding what they consider to be essential. I would then recommend constructing a statement of faith to be given to the church members and posted on the church website. A church and its community deserve to know where the church stands.

It is important to take this time for discernment because churches often draw lines between essential and non-essential issues based on tradition. Tradition is vital to the life of the church. There is a richness in how the church has traditionally conceptualized God, what it has believed about life in Christ, and how it has sought to grow in relationship with God. However, just because a church has believed or taught things for years does not mean those things are essential. Therefore, a church must evaluate its beliefs and traditions rather than uncritically accepting them.

Though this is the case, let me offer some thoughts to help the process. First, both Jesus and Paul believed certain matters were more important than others. Jesus accused the Pharisees of neglecting the "weightier matters of the law" (Mt 23:23). In Philippians 1:9–10, Paul prays that the Spirit will guide the Philippians so they can choose what is "best." Both these passages suggest that many things are important and should not be neglected and that many things are good, but not everything is weightier or best. God has placed the burden upon church leaders to discern what, among the things the church should and could be doing, is the best and most important.

I think the starting point for this endeavor is Jesus—his life, death, resurrection, and ascension. According to Paul, this is the Gospel, the "good news" (see 1 Cor 15:3–11; Phil 2:6–11). Church leaders should ask, "What is most closely connected to the Gospel?" For example, practices such as baptism and the Lord's Supper, which reenact Jesus's death, burial, and resurrection, stand extremely close to the Gospel story and should be deemed "best." While worship is closely connected to the Gospel, for the resurrected Jesus is present in the church's worship, and the church's worship is directed to and through Jesus, the age of a hymn is not closely connected to the life, death, burial, and resurrection of Jesus, though the words of the hymn might be.

Visualize this process as a set of concentric circles. At the center is the Gospel (i.e., the death, burial, resurrection, and ascension of Jesus). The next circle is the practices that stand incredibly close to the Gospel (e.g., baptism and the Lord's Supper). As you move to circles further and further removed from the Gospel, you move on to matters that, while important, become less and less weighty.

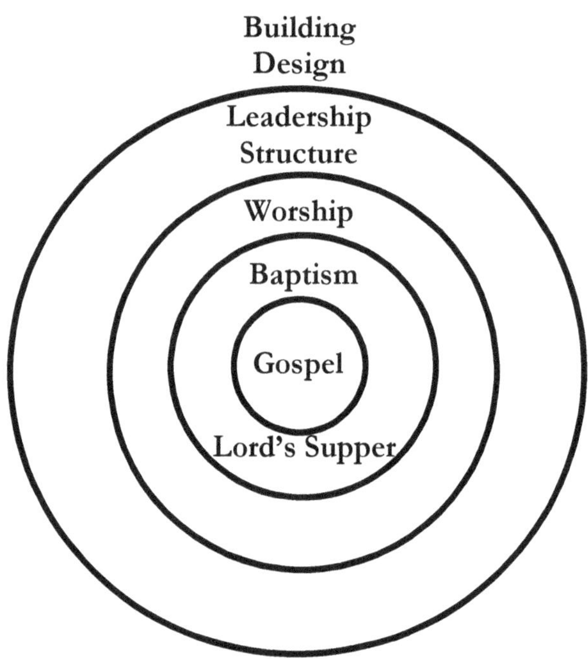

Another way to think about this process is to interpret the Bible theologically through the lens of God's story. God's story, or the story of the Bible, is the story of creation to new creation (i.e., heaven) in light of the cross. The story begins with God's creation of the heavens and the earth (Gn 1:1), and it will end with God's recreation of the universe in the "new heaven and new earth" (Is 65:17; 2 Pt 3:13; Rv 21:1). In other words, God's story is circular. It ends where it began, with the heavens and the earth as God intended them to be. What makes this story go round is Jesus's life, death, resurrection, and ascension, which Paul summarizes with the word "cross." Through the work of Jesus, God is recreating the heavens and the earth.

So any biblical passage should be interpreted with God's overall story in mind. You should ask, "How does this fit into God's story of creation to new creation in light of the cross?" For example, if you're reading through the Bible, you might notice the rampant polygamy that takes place in the Old Testament. Not only is nothing ever said against polygamy in the Old Testament, but it is also never condemned in the New Testament, at least not explicitly. So, should Christians be polygamists? Why has Christian history largely rejected polygamy in favor of monogamy?

Well, when you ask how polygamy fits into God's story from creation to new creation in light of the cross, it seems to me that it doesn't. Since God's story ends where it began, ethics are rooted in the creation. As followers of Jesus, we are to live in light of how God created and designed human beings in the beginning and what our 'new creation' lives will look like in the future. When we go back to the beginning, we find that God created Adam and Eve to live in a monogamous relationship. This was God's intention for humanity, and therefore, should reflect the lives of his people.[3]

On the flip side, consider loving your neighbor as yourself. How does the command to love your neighbor as yourself fit into God's story of creation as it develops into the new creation in light of the cross? It fits into every aspect of the story. God created the universe because of his love. God created Adam and Eve to love each other and to love and care for God's creation. Jesus came to earth and went to the cross because of love. The Bible only ever says God is one thing: "God is love" (1 Jn 4:8). Therefore, we should bind the command to love your neighbor as yourself.

I call this the "Lens of Biblical Interpretation" because when you visualize this method, it looks like a lens. The lens through which we should look at any and every biblical passage.

---

[3] N. T. Wright, *Scripture and the Authority of God: How to Read the Bible Today* (New York: HarperOne, 2013), 175–95.

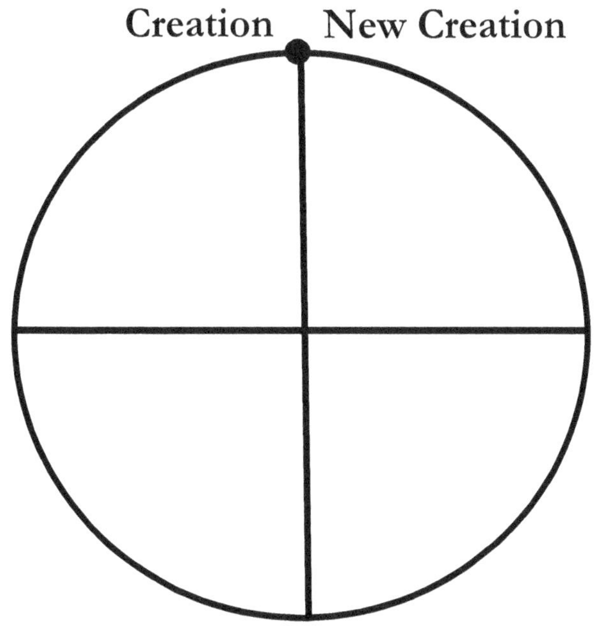

When we approach faith this way, it becomes evident that certain things don't matter. It doesn't matter who a person votes for or if they vote at all. It doesn't matter how a person interprets the difficult and gray passages of Scripture (e.g., seven literal days of creation versus seven periods of time, what heaven will look like, the operation of the Holy Spirit). It doesn't matter what a person looks like, whether they show up to church in flip flops and a t-shirt or a three-piece suit. The color of a person's skin does not matter. None of these things have any connection to the life, death, resurrection, and ascension of Jesus as seen in the story of God.

For the church to be united in purpose and person, nothing can matter other than our faith in Jesus's life, death, resurrection, and ascension and our active participation in God's story.

Paul's Thesis

Paul summarizes his way of dealing with this issue in Galatia in Galatians 3:26–29:

> For in Christ Jesus you are all children of God through faith. As many of you as were baptized into Christ have clothed yourselves with Christ. There is no longer Jew or Greek, there is no longer slave or free, there is no longer male and female; for all of you are one in Christ Jesus. And if you belong to Christ, then you are Abraham's offspring, heirs according to the promise.

Paul says that through faith in Jesus, the Galatians are all "children of God." "Children" is technically an inaccurate translation. The Greek word is "son" (*huios*), not children. Most modern translations render it children because of a desire to use gender-inclusive language. This concerns who is included and excluded in a given phrase. So, if Paul uses the word "son" but intends to include both men and women, it is translated as "children," or if Paul uses "brother" and intends the same audience, it is translated as "brothers and sisters." Gender-inclusive language is quite helpful because it better reflects the author's intent. However, this is one of the few passages where an effort to be inclusive causes us to miss a significant point Paul is making.

In this section of Galatians, Paul is talking about inheritance. Paul's understanding of inheritance stems from his Jewish roots, where inheritance was reserved for sons (i.e., males). A father gives inheritance only to his sons, not his daughters,[4] wife, or anyone else. The oldest son receives a double portion, and the remaining inheritance is divided among the remaining sons.[5] This is why it is so important in the Old Testament for a father to have a son to whom he can pass the family name and inheritance.

Paul's point in this passage is that all who place their faith in Jesus, not merely males, get to be, not children who may or may not receive an inheritance, but sons of God, rightful recipients of God's inheritance. Everyone who is baptized has clothed themselves with Christ. They are now identified with Jesus. "There is no longer Jew or Greek, there is no longer slave or free, there is no longer male and female; for all of you are one in Christ Jesus. And if you belong to Christ, then you are Abraham's offspring, heirs according to the promise."

Only Jews, not Greeks, receive a Jewish inheritance. Only free people, not slaves, receive an inheritance. Only

---

[4] The daughters of Zelophehad (Nm 36:2–12; Jos 17:3–6) are an exception where daughters and their husbands maintained temporary ownership of the inheritance until an official grandson could inherit.

[5] V. H. Matthews, "Family Relationships," in *Dictionary of the Old Testament: Pentateuch*, ed. Alexander T. Desmond and David W. Baker (Downers Grove, IL: InterVarsity Press, 2003), 295–97.

males, not females, receive an inheritance. But in Christ Jesus, we all become one. There is no distinction between Jew and Greek, slave and free, or male and female. All are equal sons of God, able to receive the inheritance of salvation from God.[6]

However, there is an important caveat. When Paul says there is no longer a distinction, he is not saying that everyone becomes exactly the same, morphing into one another and losing individual identity. Jews are still Jews. Gentiles are still Gentiles. Males are still males. Females are still females. Rather, Paul is advocating for unity within diversity. Jews bring important things to the table, and so do Gentiles. Males bring important things to the table, and so do females. Each person brings something unique and must be allowed to be their unique self (see Rom 12:4–8; 1 Cor 12:12–31; Eph 4:11–16).[7]

However, Paul believes that this realization changes how we treat one another. A perfect example in Galatians is the fruit of the Spirit (Gal 5:22–26). Note that all the

---

[6] My development of this interpretation is indebted to conversations with John Mark Hicks.

[7] The role of slaves and slave masters is a different conversation that goes well beyond the purposes of this book. Briefly, I will say that I in no way condone the practice of owning another human being. I firmly believe that the foundation of the Gospel and the story of God make owning another image-bearer of God impossible. Although Scripture does not ever speak against slavery and many times condones it, I do not believe that the story of God, as seen in Jesus's life, death, burial, resurrection, and ascension, can be construed to support such an unethical practice. Therefore, there is nothing that a slave-master relationship can positively bring to the church.

descriptors relate to how we treat one another. In Christ, we love, have patience, and display self-control with one another.

Our Culture

How can the modern church cultivate a culture of personal unity?

We Are All "Sons" of God

It begins with recognizing that everyone who places their faith in Jesus is a "son" of God and receives an inheritance of salvation. In other words, faith in Jesus is what matters. The common ground that unites the church is faith in the life, death, resurrection, and ascension of Jesus, not what one might believe about creation, the Holy Spirit, women's roles, or heaven.

The church that Jesus established is meant to reflect unity within diversity. The modern church must discover a way to be unified by our faith in Jesus and be able to disagree about issues that are farther away from the center of our faith (i.e., the life, death, resurrection, and ascension of Jesus). This does not mean that every church must look the same. On the contrary, part of the diversity within the church is the diversity of churches that come from different traditions, have different styles of worship, and can do different things in the world as a continuation of God's story. However, these differences cannot be allowed to divide and separate those within a congregation or between congregations. Rather, we celebrate the diversity within the church in the same manner we celebrate the diversity within God's entire creation. The church catholic comes together, despite differences, to carry out God's mission in the world and our individual communities.

Individuality Is Important

While faith unites the church, it does not negate the importance of individual contributions. Individually, people will vote, interpret passages, think, and dress differently. There must be respect for other people's individuality and the unique contributions each person can bring to the table to strengthen the church.

You might even learn something from people who think and do things differently. I believe debating is vital to a healthy culture and healthy community. The word "debate" has a negative connotation in our society. When you think of debating, you likely think of two people on TV yelling at each other over political or sports opinions. That's not what I mean when I say "debate." Instead, I mean a healthy conversation where two sides express their different opinions, lay out their individual arguments, and thoughtfully consider the other person's perspective. No yelling. No anger. Just a conversation characterized by more listening than speaking. In the end, the two sides don't have to agree. It's perfectly fine to agree to disagree, but we do have to show respect.

Such debates, or conversations, are what carry a culture and community forward because they allow a culture to learn and grow from one another. Growth does not occur when we are in our comfort zone. You cannot grow a muscle by keeping it comfortable and resting, but you must put that muscle under stress, pushing it to its limit. Similarly, our beliefs and practices must be challenged, questioned, and pushed out of their comfort zone. The good ones will prevail, and the bad or poorly thought-through ones will be forced to change.

When was the last time your church brought in a speaker to present a viewpoint which was different than that held by the majority of your congregation? When was the last time two of your congregation members were allowed to make a presentation based on opposite interpretations of a passage? When was the last time you facilitated a church-wide or small-group-led discussion where people could express differing opinions?

Live by the Fruit of the Spirit

At the end of the day, we must simply cultivate cultures filled with the fruit of the Spirit—love, joy, peace, patience, kindness, goodness, faithfulness, gentleness, and self-control. Imagine a world where churches could facilitate conversations about differing opinions filled with these qualities. Imagine a world where different churches, with different traditions and practices, could come together and participate in God's story while displaying these characteristics. This is the type of world God desires for his people!

This process begins with church leaders. Leaders must model for their congregation what it looks like to disagree while still displaying the fruit of the Spirit (see chapter 6, above, on imitation). When your congregation gets on social media or watches TV, all they see are debates without the Spirit. The church must show people a different way to disagree and debate in the way of God's Spirit.

5

Ephesus
A Culture of New Creation

Up to this point, we have discussed aspects necessary for any good culture, whether that be a church culture, sports team culture, or business culture. However, there is something special about the church. The church might have similarities to a sports team or business, but it is quite unique from them. Therefore, certain things are necessary for a good, Spirit-powered church culture that are not for other cultures. Indeed, there are aspects of a good, Spirit-powered church culture that other cultures are not even capable of cultivating.

The Church in Ephesus

We see one such aspect of cultivating a church culture in Ephesians. Ephesians is a letter Paul wrote in the early 60s while in prison in Rome.[1] Paul says he is writing this letter

---

[1] There is much scholarly debate about where Paul was in prison when writing the prison epistles (i.e., Ephesians, Philippians, Colossians, and Philemon). The historical interpretation is that Paul was in prison in Rome, though more recent scholarship has made a solid argument for Paul's imprisonment in Ephesus. The location of

"to the saints who are in Ephesus and are faithful in Christ Jesus" (Eph 1:1). However, the phrase "in Ephesus" is not original,[2] having been added by a scribe copying the letter sometime after Paul. Therefore, Paul's original letter did not have an addressee.[3]

Reading through Ephesians, you'll notice, unlike in Paul's other letters, that he does not deal with any specific issues. Instead, he broadly talks about the faith, life, and unity of the church.[4] Within this context, one of the major

---

Paul's imprisonment determines the dating of the letter. If he was in prison in Rome, then Ephesians would be dated to the early 60s. If in Ephesus, then the letter would date earlier. Jeannine K. Brown, "The Letter to the Philippians," in *Dictionary of Paul and His Letters: A Compendium of Contemporary Biblical Scholarship*, ed. Scot McKnight (Downers Grove, IL: IVP Academic, 2023), 809–10. For an argument favoring an Ephesian imprisonment, see N. Gupta and M. Bird, *Philippians*, NCBC (Cambridge: Cambridge University Press, 2020).

[2] Andrew T. Lincoln, *Ephesians*, Word Biblical Commentary 42 (Dallas, TX: Word Books, 1990), 1–2.

[3] There have been a variety of explanations regarding the origin and original audience of the letter. I believe it is possible that Ephesians was originally a circular letter meant for multiple churches in Asia Minor, including Ephesus. I believe this best explains the general nature of the letter. Unlike his other letters, Paul does not address specific people or issues in the church to which he is writing. For a development of this interpretation, see J. B. Lightfoot, "The Destination of the Epistle to the Ephesians," in *Biblical Essays* (London: Macmillan, 1893), 375–96. Another possible interpretation is that the original letter included a recipient that was lost or changed; see Lincoln, *Ephesians*, 3–4.

[4] Lincoln, *Ephesians*, lxxiv.

emphases in Ephesians is that the church, unlike other groups and cultures, has a culture of new creation.

God had a plan before the creation of the world to deal with the problem of sin and create a people for himself. This plan, a "mystery" until it was revealed "in the fulness of time," was to "gather up all things in [Jesus], things in heaven and things on earth" (Eph 1:9–10). Throughout the Bible, heaven refers to the place where God is, and earth to the place we are. In the beginning (see Gn 1–2), heaven and earth were the same. God and humanity occupied the same space; they lived and dwelled together in perfect harmony.[5]

When sin entered creation (Gn 3), it separated humanity from God. Heaven and earth were no longer the same, though they still overlapped. One could see and experience the overlap of heaven and earth in the Old Testament at the tabernacle and later the temple, specifically at the ark of the covenant where God dwelled among his people on the mercy seat. In the New Testament, one sees and experiences the overlap of heaven and earth through the Holy Spirit, prayer, the Lord's Supper, and most importantly, in Jesus, God coming to tabernacle among us (Jn 1:14).

However, God's plan is not for heaven and earth to merely overlap, but for them to become the same once again, "to gather up all things in [Jesus], things in heaven and things

---

[5] In his book *The Lost World of Genesis One*, John Walton argues that the story of Genesis 1 is God's creation of a cosmic temple. The cosmos was meant to be God's temple (i.e., dwelling place) where God dwelled with his creation. John H. Walton, *The Lost World of Genesis One*, vol. 2, Ancient Cosmology and the Origins Debate (Downers Grove, IL: IVP Academic, 2009).

on earth." It is for us to return to Eden, where God and humanity occupy the same space. The Bible begins with the words, "In the beginning God created the heavens and the earth" (Gn 1:1). The ultimate vision of God, given in both the Old and New Testament, is the creation of "a new heaven and a new earth" (Is 65:17; 2 Pt 3:13; Rv 21:1).

The problem God must overcome to bring heaven and earth together is evil. Specifically in Ephesians, Paul speaks of the evil forces in the "heavenlies" (literal Greek translation), or as most English translations render it, "heavenly places." The easiest way to conceptualize what Paul is speaking about is with our typical understanding of Satan, an evil spiritual being who works counter to God's plan and influences humanity. However, it must be acknowledged that 'Satan' is a vast oversimplification of what Paul is speaking about in Ephesians. Paul does not have in mind one singular evil being who is controlling all the evil forces and trying to spoil God's plan. However, our typical conception is a reasonable place to start understanding Paul's language of spiritual beings in Ephesians.[6]

The important point that we should take from Ephesians is that Paul believes that while these evil forces exist in the heavenlies, they still impact life on earth.[7] Behind much of the evil on earth and many powerful people and institutions are the forces of evil in the heavenlies. So Paul can say

---

[6] For a deeper dive into spiritual beings in the Bible, check out my podcast series on the spiritual realm at thinkingtheologically.org.

[7] N. T. Wright, *Paul and His Letter to the Ephesians*, Logos Mobile Education (Waukesha, WI: The Wisconsin Center for Christian Study, 2019).

things like, before the Ephesians chose to follow Jesus, they were following "the ruler of the power of the air" (Eph 2:2) and that "our struggle is not against enemies of blood and flesh, but against the rulers, against the authorities, against the cosmic powers of this present darkness, against the spiritual forces of evil in the heavenly places" (Eph 6:12).

So the problem is the spiritual forces of evil. The ultimate solution is the bringing together of heaven and earth. How does God bring about this solution? Paul's answer: Jesus. Jesus redeems from sin (Eph 1:7–8a), he has taken authority over the powers in the heavenlies (Eph 1:20–21), and Jesus's triumph has been declared, through the church, to the heavenly powers (Eph 3:10).

Since God has defeated sin and the powers of evil, he can unite heaven and earth. God will do this, once and for all, when Jesus returns and establishes the new heaven and new earth. However, in the meantime, God has already begun uniting heaven and earth in the church. The church is where one can see and experience the overlap of heaven and earth in a community filled with God's Spirit. This means that the church's culture must be characterized by new creation.

The Church as New Creation

Dwelling Place of God

Cultivating a culture of new creation begins with recognizing that the church is the new dwelling place of God. Speaking of the church, Paul says in Ephesians 2:21–22, "In [Jesus] the whole structure is joined together and grows into a holy temple in the Lord; in whom you also are built together spiritually into a dwelling place for God." Paul says that the church is a "holy temple" and "a dwelling place for God," the place where heaven and earth overlap.

Notice that Paul does not say we instantaneously become God's dwelling place, but that we "grow" and are "built together" into this dwelling place. When people follow Jesus, they are filled with God through the Holy Spirit. God is present when the church gathers together in worship, fellowship, or to take the Lord's Supper. However, as a person grows in their faith and spends more time with God, or as a church grows in their active participation in God's story, the more in tune that individual or church becomes with God. They open themselves up more to God's Spirit and God's presence. In this way, both individuals and churches continue growing into God's dwelling place.

This means that churches must cultivate cultures that allow the church and its members to grow into God's dwelling place. Such cultures will seek to be in tune with God's will, making decisions through the discernment of God's Spirit. These cultures will emphasize dwelling with Jesus around the Lord's Table, the movement of God's Spirit through the words of Scripture, and fellowship with the people of God.

Most importantly, such cultures will be cultures of love. In Ephesians 3:18–19, Paul prays that the Ephesians will come to know "the breadth and length and height and depth" of Christ's love so that they "may be filled with the fullness of God." A church is filled with the presence of God only inasmuch as they are filled with Christ's love. A church that does not love or fails to love people who look different, live different lifestyles, commit specific sins, believe certain theologies, or participate in certain Christian traditions is a church that is not filled with the fullness of God.

The church as God's dwelling place inherently presents the church as both internally and externally focused. The church is internally focused because it is in the church where God is most fully experienced. God can be experienced on a mountaintop as a person soaks in God's glorious creation or at a small-town coffee shop, but God is experienced more fully in the church. The presence of God in the church's worship and Jesus's presence around the Lord's Table is a presence that supersedes the experience of God in other places.

So, the church's identity begins with its practices in the presence of God. The question is, how does your church emphasize God's presence? Is the Lord's Supper a quick moment to get through, or is it a time to sit in the presence of Jesus? Is your worship an appeal to entertain your community in hopes of gaining more members, or is it an intimate conversation between God and his people? Are times of fellowship tacked on to the "more important" aspects of church to try and keep people engaged, or is it a time for Spirit-filled people to engage their callings together?

Additionally, Paul says in Galatians 6:10 that we are to do good, "especially for those of the family of faith." I think one of the reasons Paul says this is that we learn how to do good and to love by loving the people of the church. If we cannot love the people we go to church with every week, the people we share deep convictions with about

Jesus, how can we be expected to love anyone else? The church is also where we practice love because our love for one another allows us to fail at love without ruining the relationship. We can get back up and try again.

The church's identity begins with its practices in the presence of God and its mutual love, but it does not end here. When the church encounters the living God of the entire world, it is convicted to actively participate in God's worldwide story. Rather than keeping God to themselves in the comfort of their auditoriums, the church is charged to go out to the world and make disciples (Mt 28:19–20). They are reminded, as Israel was, that God is the God of the entire world (Ex 19:5). They learn to love in the church so that they can go out and love the people of the world created in the image of God.

Too many churches operate like a country club. Access to the church is only for certain people who look a certain way and believe certain things. They may not tell someone who fails to meet these qualifications to leave, but their welcoming of them into their community will make it clear that they don't belong. They do things to benefit themselves, make their members happy, and build up their church numbers, name, and brand rather than being for the benefit of the world.

Let's get one thing straight: the church is not a country club. The church does not exist for itself. The church does not have closed doors only opened with a secret password. The church is the community of the God of the whole world. The church exists for the world. The church has doors wide open for the world, sinners, and outcasts to walk through and find meaning, purpose, love, and community. The church's identity might begin inside, with an encounter with God, but it does not belong inside but out in the world, actively participating in God's worldwide story.

Dream Big

Since God dwells in the church, the church is empowered by God. Paul says in Ephesians 1:19–20:

> … and what is the immeasurable greatness of [God's] power for us who believe, according to the working of his great power. God put this power to work in Christ when he raised him from the dead and seated him at his right hand in the heavenly places.

Paul uses three words for power in these two verses. First, he speaks of the "immeasurable greatness of [God's] power," the word power here is *dynamis*, from which we get the English word dynamite. While it would be incorrect to interpret Paul as speaking of God's dynamite-like power, it does show the intensity with which Paul speaks of God's power. Second, Paul says that God's power is "working," the Greek word *energeia*, from which we get the English word energy. Finally, Paul speaks of God's "great power," the Greek word *kratos*, referring to God's might or strength. This great power and might is seen most fully when God raised Jesus from the dead.

It is this power that God works on the church's behalf. Power to which the church has access. Paul says in Ephesians 3:20–21:

> Now to him who by the power at work within us is able to accomplish abundantly far more than all we can ask or imagine, to him be glory in the church and in Christ Jesus to all generations, forever and ever. Amen.

Since the church has access to God's power, God is able to do within the church "abundantly far more than all we can ask or imagine."

Therefore, churches must cultivate cultures that dream big. Cultures that dream not by worldly standards but by God's standards. Dreams that do not reside on the power present among the members of the church but on the power of God at work within the church. Cultivating a culture of new creation means churches must begin doing things they know, without a shadow of a doubt, they will not be able to accomplish unless God shows up.

Notice also that Paul says that God's power in the church produces glory "to all generations, forever and ever." God's power and glory are not something the church only possessed in the past; they are something the church possesses in the present and will continue to possess into the future. We can have confidence in the church's future because we are confident that God's power will always be displayed in the church. In other words, we don't have to rely on our power to move the church into the future. We rely on the power of God in the Holy Spirit.

New Humanity

To repeat the point made in the last two chapters, a culture of new creation is a culture of unity in both purpose and people because a new creation culture consists of a new humanity. Paul says that Jesus has created a new humanity, uniting Jews and Gentiles "to God in one body through the cross" (Eph 2:15–16). This means that salvation is not individualistic.

In the contemporary church, most Christians seem to think that salvation is all about them. Jesus saves me, and Jesus saves you as individuals. However, Paul argues that Jesus doesn't save you and me. Instead, Jesus saves us collectively, together, as one body. Jesus first reconciles human beings to one another in the church and then reconciles all of us, the entire church, to God (see chapter 7 on reconciliation).

Christianity isn't an individualistic religion. Certainly, an individual can have a relationship with God, and there are responsibilities that individual Christians have, particularly moral responsibilities. However, God did not intend for people to follow Jesus on their own but to follow Jesus within a community (more on this in chapter 6).

New Self

The church, as the dwelling place of God, not only consists of a new humanity but also new people. Ephesians 4:22–24 says that we are to put away our old self and way of life to put on a new self that is "created according to the likeness of God in true righteousness and holiness." As the dwelling place of God, the church ought to look like God.

If God is truly present within a church, then by necessity, God is changing that church to look more like him. Church leaders must consistently push their members to change their lives and thoughts to better reflect the image of God.

God creates humanity in his image because human beings are meant to be God's royal representatives.[8] Think of human beings as God's mirror, meant to reflect God out into the creation. However, sin cracks humanity's mirror. Human beings still reflect God but not perfectly, as a broken mirror can still reflect an imperfect image. Anytime a person does good, they are living out of the part of themselves that is created in God's image. The Spirit then restores our image-bearing ability by fixing the cracks in our mirror so we can better reflect God's image. Therefore, if the Spirit is present, the church should reflect God.

What is your church reflecting? Are you reflecting yourself? Are you reflecting the business strategies of the world? Are you reflecting the music and shows valued by the world? Many churches talk about God but reflect something else. They are built around the personality of the minister rather than God. They operate based on the business strategies the elders have implemented in their work rather than the power of the Holy Spirit. Their beliefs and practices reflect their favorite political party rather than God's creative purpose. Churches must reflect the image of God.

---

[8] Gordon J. Wenham, *Genesis 1-15*, Word Biblical Commentary 1 (Waco, TX: Word Books, 1987), 26–34.

Armor of God

While God dwells in the church, the church still dwells in the world. A world still under the influence of the powers of evil in the heavenlies, though Jesus has won the victory. However, the church is not on its own to battle against these evil forces but has been given the armor of God (Eph 6:10–17).

Paul believes that sin and evil work on at least two levels. The first was mentioned earlier and is his emphasis in Ephesians. That is, spiritual forces of evil exist in the spiritual realm that impact life on earth. I said the easiest way to think about this is with our typical conception of Satan, though Paul's point is much more complex. We typically think of Satan as tempting us to do things that don't reflect God's image and doing things that oppose God's design (e.g., poverty, racism, abuse).

Second, Paul believes in capital-S Sin.[9] A little-s sin is when you or I, as individuals, miss the mark, the literal definition of the Greek word for sin. However, there are things in the world we would say are the result of sin that cannot be traced back to one individual missing the mark. For example, worldwide poverty results from sin, but no one person is responsible for poverty. This is a capital-S Sin. Such Sin is a force that works in the world and upon human beings. When human beings sin, they contribute to Sin and are influenced by it. This is why, in places such as Romans 5:12–

---

[9] Beverly Roberts Gaventa, *When in Romans: An Invitation to Linger with the Gospel According to Paul*, Theological Explorations for the Church Catholic (Grand Rapids, MI: Baker Academic, 2018).

21, Paul can personify Sin and talk about it doing things like setting up a kingdom.

In a world where we must battle against spiritual forces of evil and Sin, we need protection to keep our mirrors from being further cracked. Our protection is the armor of God. We have the belt of truth and breastplate of righteousness that guide our thoughts, actions, and decisions. We have shoes that guide us in our efforts to go out into the world and spread the love and presence of God. We have the shield of faith and helmet of salvation, whereby we place our complete trust in God to deliver us and eventually defeat all evil. Finally, we have the sword of the word of God, which, like when Jesus was tempted in the wilderness, we use to combat the lies and temptations of Sin.

So we must equip our congregations with the armor of God. We must teach the truth of God's word so that they can strap on their sword with a belt. We must constantly remind them that they have been made righteous. They are in a right relationship with God because of what Jesus did for them on the cross, so they need to live based on this new identity. We must provide training and resources that people can use as shoes to share their faith. As leaders, we need to provide a model of what it looks like to stand against sin with the power God provides through his armor rather than self-reliance.

6

Philippi
A Culture of Imitation

There are four primary ways people learn new information. These four ways are an oversimplification of how all human beings come to learn new things, but they do provide a good generalization to understand how learning occurs. Some people are auditory learners; they learn through hearing. For example, if an auditory learner is learning to build a desk, they can just hear someone explain it. Others are visual learners; they learn through seeing. They need to see someone build the desk. Others learn through reading and writing; they read the instructions for building the desk. Finally, some people are kinesthetic learners; they learn by doing. They need to get the desk parts in their hands and start working with them.

It is likely that no one falls perfectly into any of these categories. A person might gravitate toward one and learn best through that method but can likely learn in other ways as well. You might even recognize that you learn different types of information better in different ways. You may learn facts best through hearing but how to build something best kinesthetically.

Now, think about how information is typically taught in churches. How does the church help people learn new information? New things about God? New ways to live by the Spirit? New ways to engage the community and world?

The majority of churches have their greatest success in auditory learning. They do a great deal of preaching and teaching, generally lecture-style. Many churches also succeed in reading and writing. Christian communities are formed and shaped through the word of God, and a great deal of Bible reading takes place in most churches. As Bible reading and preaching occur, many people who learn through reading and writing will take notes to help them comprehend what is being taught. I would even argue that many churches do a decent job facilitating kinesthetic learning, though there is plenty of room for churches to grow in this area. Anytime a church offers a way for people to live out their faith in the real world, it is a form of kinesthetic learning. Service projects, small groups, and fellowship activities allow people to experience a hands-on way to learn and understand what it means to live as a follower of Jesus.

I believe the area of learning most churches struggle with is visual learning. How do you facilitate people in your congregation "seeing" faith? Perhaps, every once in a while, you show a video. Perhaps you have a graphic that goes with different themes and sermon series to help people visualize the concepts. However, I believe there is so much room for churches to improve in visual learning and that one of the best ways for people to visualize their faith is through mentorship.

When people build relationships with those older and wiser in the faith, it provides them not only with people they can speak to and glean wisdom but also with people they can watch. They can see how that person lives out their faith in the real world and amid real-life difficulties and traumas and imitate that in their own life. It is this type of imitation that Paul emphasizes as a key to cultivating a Spirit-powered church culture in his letter to the Philippians.

Imitation Culture in Philippi

Philippians was written by Paul and traditionally was believed to have been written around 62 CE, while he was imprisoned in Rome.[1] It was written to the predominantly Gentile church in Philippi,[2] which Paul established alongside Silas and Timothy in 48–49 CE. This is probably Paul's most heartfelt letter, written to help the Philippians, who were dealing with several issues. They are being persecuted by pagans, influenced by Judaizers pushing circumcision, and there is some internal strife (e.g., Euodia and Syntyche [Phil 4:2]).

To deal with these issues, Paul gives the Philippians some examples, or some mentors, to imitate—himself and, most importantly, Jesus. Paul firmly believes that the Philippians need mentors to stay faithful in their current difficult circumstances. Paul sums this up perfectly in Philippians

---

[1] As mentioned in the previous chapter, there is debate regarding the location of Paul's imprisonment when writing the prison epistles.

[2] Brown, "The Letter to the Philippians," 809.

3:17: "Brothers and sisters, join in imitating me, and observe those who live according to the example you have in us."

Timothy

Paul's emphasis on imitation is rooted in the culture of mentorship Paul cultivated in his personal life. This is seen perhaps nowhere better than in Paul's relationship with Timothy. Timothy is Paul's younger companion. He helped Paul establish the church in Philippi and is introduced as a co-author of this letter (Phil 1:1). In Philippians 2:19–24, Paul speaks of Timothy, saying that he hopes to send him to the Philippians soon because Timothy is the only one not seeking his own interests, and "like a son with a father he has served with me in the work of the gospel."

One of the primary ways a child learns, particularly a young child, is through imitation of their parents. A child learns to speak by imitating the sounds their parents make. Children begin learning new facial expressions by imitating their parents. Even a grown adult does things or speaks in ways that imitate their parents. For example, I have been told my whole life that I preach like my grandfather. Since I grew up listening to him preach, when I began preaching, I naturally imitated the preaching style I had heard my entire life.

A popular country song since its release in 2006 is "I've Been Watching You," by Rodney Atkins. The song begins with a father driving through town with his young son, who's eating a Happy Meal. When the father slams on his brakes, the son's food goes flying, and he says a bad word beginning with "s." The father asks his son where he learned that word, and the son replies, "I've been watching you."

The next verse begins with the father praying for himself and his son. Later that night, before going to bed, his son gets on his knees and begins praying. The father asks, "Where'd you learn to pray like that?" The son replies, "I've been watching you."

A son learns, for good or bad, from imitating his father. Paul built this reality into his ministry. He brought young Timothy along, as a father might bring his son along, so that Timothy could watch him, learn from him, and ultimately imitate him. As we see in 1 and 2 Timothy, this allows Timothy to grow into an important leader in the church in Ephesus.

Like Paul, we can begin cultivating father-son cultural relationships in our churches by simply bringing people along, and this begins with church leaders. When you go and visit someone who's sick, bring someone along with you. When you teach a Bible class, ask someone to be your assistant. I have even known eldership groups who have asked potential elders to sit in on elder meetings to learn what it's like to be an elder and how a healthy eldership should function. Cultivating a culture of imitators begins with simply bringing people along.

Paul

With such an understanding, Paul presents himself to the Philippians as a mentor to be imitated. Paul opens the letter by discussing his imprisonment (Phil 1:12–30). He does so to hold himself out as an example for the Philippians to imitate as they deal with their own persecution. Paul says that while one might expect his imprisonment to hinder his spreading of the Gospel, it has actually helped. It has encouraged other Christians to follow his example and preach the Gospel with more boldness. So the Philippians shouldn't view their persecution as a sign that the Gospel is ineffective or that God's plans have been thwarted. On the contrary, like Paul, they should allow God to use their persecution as an opportunity to spread the Gospel and demonstrate its power.

The reality of life is that it is hard. We face a lot of difficult things, forcing us to ask: How do I respond as a follower of Jesus? How do I respond to another school shooting? How do I respond when I lose someone near and dear to me? How do I respond when I'm diagnosed with cancer? How do I respond when my marriage is on the rocks or my child is rebelling?

When we face any of these issues, especially for the first time, it is daunting because we have no idea what to do. However, our churches are filled with people who have already gone through just about anything imaginable. People who can provide insight into how to faithfully deal with whatever a person is going through.

I want to key in on the idea of "faithfully" dealing with something. As followers of Jesus, our response to difficult circumstances should not be to merely make it through by the skin of our teeth or to deal with it in any way we can. Instead, our response should be to handle the situation faithfully in the manner of Jesus. This is where Christian mentors are so important. They can provide insight into not just how to deal with something but how to deal with it as a follower of Jesus. They can tell us what to do and what not to do in a way that is true to our faith.

Generally, a person can glean such wisdom by simply asking someone. Most people are willing to share their stories if asked, but for a person to know they need to ask means they have gotten to know someone well enough to begin learning their story. They have spent significant time speaking with and developing relationships with people older and more mature than themselves.

Paul moves on in Philippians to present himself as an example of valuing citizenship in heaven rather than the world. In Philippians 3:2–11, Paul talks about gaining something from God through Judaism and the Jewish law. He says that he's an example of someone who should be able to boast in Judaism. Before following Jesus, Paul had everything one could desire within Judaism. He lists seven attributes, perhaps metaphorically to say his list is complete.[3] There is nothing that could be added. Paul has every reason to boast, yet he gave everything up, literally losing all he had, to follow Jesus. Not only does Paul say he lost everything, but he's actually glad he did. He says it was all "rubbish," literally "dung" or "excrement." Dung is the value Paul places on his Jewish roots compared to knowing Jesus and being known by him.

Like Paul, we live in a world where the people we see on TV and social media, those we can imitate, tend to value the wrong things. They value money, particular careers, cars,

---

[3] N. T. Wright, "Paul and His Letter to the Philippians: Small Group Edition" (Online Course, Udemy, n.d.).

houses; and they value relationships with unrealistic expectations based on unchristian principles and present themselves one way online but exist entirely differently in reality. The problem is that when this is all we see, it is also what we end up imitating.

This is why being present at church, being engaged with the church, and getting to know the people of the church is so important. It gives us other people to see and imitate. It presents us with a concrete, visual example of another way to live and do life.

This also means that we, particularly church leaders, must be people worthy of imitation. We must live in such a way that people can look at us and see something different than they see in the world. Our congregations need to look at us and see someone who does not value worldly things or success but the things of God. They need to see what it looks like to not value or rely upon our personal ability, strengths, or weaknesses, but rather on the power of God at work within us through the Spirit.

However, as a follower of Jesus, Paul knows that he has not yet attained full perfection. So, he forgets what lies behind (i.e., his former life in Judaism) and strains forward toward his heavenly prize (Phil 3:12–16). The imagery Paul uses is of a Greek foot race. When athletes run a race, they cannot run by looking back at the starting line; they must run by looking forward to the finish line. So, Paul runs his Christian race by not looking back to what he had and lost but by looking forward toward the finishing line of salvation. He lives in such a way as not to go backward but to move forward towards looking like Jesus.

Surrounding ourselves with people who are older, wiser, and more mature in the faith gives us something to pursue, as we desire to become wise and mature like them. If we are only ever surrounded by people less faithfully mature than ourselves, we may be tempted to think we are good, that we have already obtained maturity, and that there is no reason to continue growing. However, being surrounded by more mature people reminds us that there is still work to be done.

A similar phenomenon is seen in sports. If an athlete only ever plays against players worse than them, then they will stop developing and becoming a better athlete. For athletes to develop, they must challenge and stretch themselves by competing against players better than them. They train with the mindset that there are other players out there just as good as them, and if they don't train harder, they will be passed by. In our Christian race or athletic event, mentors are the people who push us to continue growing and developing in our faith.

Paul's final statement about himself as a mentor is found in Philippians 4:8–9:

> Finally, beloved, whatever is true, whatever is honorable, whatever is just, whatever is pure, whatever is pleasing, whatever is commendable, if there is any excellence and if there is anything worthy of praise, think about these things. Keep on doing the things that you have learned and received and heard and seen in me, and the God of peace will be with you.

Paul implies that the things that are good and worthy of praise, which the Philippians should set their minds on, are not only things they learned from Paul but also things they saw Paul value.

Paul says we are to value anything that is true, honorable, and commendable. He does not say we only value things in the church, our family, things done by Christians, or things spoken by a particular political party. Anything and everything good should be celebrated. The problem is that the world does a poor job of determining what is good.

The world often gets good backward, calling good evil and evil good. Abortion is good; religion is bad. People need mentors to show them what is worth celebrating and what is not. They need mentors to celebrate their good accomplishments and hold them accountable for their mistakes.

Jesus

Finally, the most important person that the Philippians are to imitate is Jesus. Likely, the second most well-known passage in Philippians is the Christ Hymn in Philippians 2:6–11. In this passage, Paul seems to be dealing with the internal problems in Philippi. He responds by saying that the Philippians should be unified, of the same mind, and look to the interests of others rather than one's own (Phil 2:2–4). He then quotes this early Christian worship song to show that Jesus is an example of looking to other's interests rather than one's own. In the same way that Jesus left his place in heaven to become a "slave" and give his life to save others, the Philippians should also give of themselves to benefit others.

Our greatest mentor is Jesus. At the end of the day, Jesus is the one we should strive to imitate. The age-old question, "What would Jesus do?," is still relevant.

In the church today, we can get too bogged down with ethical concerns and debates. What does Paul mean when he says women should keep silent? Do we have to keep the Old Testament commandments condemning homosexual behavior? How do we apply Jesus's teachings about divorce?

These questions are essential for the church to consider, talk about, and ultimately apply to their practice of following Jesus. However, I do not believe any of these or similar questions should be the starting or ending point of Christian ethics. There are many questions the church will and should consider that do not have a clear-cut answer. Instead, the starting and ending point of Christian life and ethics should be Jesus's life. If the church started with imitating Jesus's life in their own lives and then moved to deeper ethical issues, I firmly believe the church would be in a much better place.

The problem is that many churches don't want to do what Jesus did. They don't want to eat with tax collectors and sinners like Jesus. They don't want to touch the lepers Jesus touched. They don't want to spend time with the poor, outcast, and disadvantaged like Jesus. They don't want to flip the tables of the rich and powerful like Jesus. They don't want to call out the religious hypocrisy present among the religious elite like Jesus.

Many churches would rather spend their time screaming about women's roles, homosexuality, and divorce than living like Jesus because it allows them to place themselves on their ethical high horse. It allows them to present themselves as the ethical elite, looking down on everyone else who are "sinners" because they don't subscribe to their church's theology. Let's remember, though, that Jesus's ministry humbled the religious elite and ate with the "sinners."

I am not saying this to take any kind of theological stance or to say that churches should not take ethical stances on these issues. On the contrary, I believe these issues are essential for churches to discuss and that many churches' failure to address such issues has allowed the culture of the world to become the culture of the church. I believe it is the job of ministers and church leaders to facilitate these difficult conversations based on biblical principles and convictions. I believe churches can and should be united regardless of how they interpret biblical passages on many ethical issues. However, I do not believe such questions should be the starting or ending point of the church's life. The starting and ending point is imitating the church's greatest mentor, Jesus.

Conclusion

How does the church cultivate a culture of mentorship and imitation? Here are a couple of suggestions, though far from a comprehensive list.

Small Groups

Establish intergenerational small groups. Such groups allow Christians of different ages and different spiritual maturity levels to talk and interact with one another. There are many different ways a church can establish small groups, each dependent on the purpose of the groups. For example, if a church uses small groups as an evangelistic tool, then groups based on age might be the best option. However, if a church establishes small groups to cultivate a culture of imitation, the groups must be intergenerational.

I would recommend that these groups regularly do two things. First, study scripture together. The study material could be a continuation of the sermon, sermon-adjacent material, a book, or following the lectionary. Bible study allows multiple generations to consider the meaning of passages together, to discuss what those passages mean to them, and to discern how they can be applied to real-world situations based on different people's personal experiences.

Second, the groups need to spend time in fellowship. Too many small groups engage in Bible study only. People come together, study the Bible, and then leave. This is not wrong, but it misses the fullness that small groups can become. When people are allowed to share a meal together, it sparks conversations about their lives. These conversations open the opportunity for people to seek spiritual advice from those who have dealt with similar things.

Assistants

One of the easiest ways to cultivate a culture of imitation is for ministers to bring people along as assistants. If you are a youth minister and someone in your youth group is interested in ministry, allow that person to help you teach and plan events. If you are a preacher and someone in your congregation is interested in preaching and teaching, ask them to co-teach or co-preach with you. You can even work on the sermon or class together. If your church has the funds, bring in a summer intern. When you go visit the sick, bring members along with you. It is not just the minister's job to visit people; it is the job of the entire church. If you see people express interest or show giftedness in an area you do not work in (e.g., children's ministry or technology), pair them with someone who works in that area.

College Program

If your church is near a college, create a program that pairs college students with couples in your church. Many college students would love such a program. It gives them people to rely on when a problem arises and they are far from home. The couples can invite their students over for meals, and college students never refuse a free meal! More than this, it gives students, who are in a challenging and crucial transitional stage in life, mentors they can learn from and imitate.

Live a Spirit-Filled Life

Perhaps the best way to cultivate a culture of imitation is to live a Spirit-filled life worthy of imitation. Ministers and church leaders are the ones people look up to, whether you like it or not. You are the people up in front of the congregation regularly, the voice and face of your church. Therefore, you must live in a way worthy of the imitation of your congregation and community. As St. Francis of Assisi said, "Preach the gospel at all times. Use words if necessary." Remember, James says that as leaders and teachers, we will be judged more strictly (Jas 3:1).

This is especially true for those working with young people. Young people tend to be more impressionable and in more need of good mentors to imitate. Many young people you will encounter do not have the best mentors at home or in school and will rely on the good images they get from people in their church. A good mentor who provides a positive image and relationship to a young person could set that individual on a path of faithfulness and success that would otherwise be unavailable.

7

Colossae
A Culture of Reconciliation

Perhaps the most unique aspect of church culture is that the church is not merely a gathering of like-minded individuals pursuing similar goals, but is also a family. At least, the church is supposed to be a family! Paul uses a derivative of the Greek noun "brother" 142 times throughout his letters, demonstrating that for Paul, the church's identity is that they have become the new family of God.

There are a couple of reasons that this is significant. First, Paul lived in a communal society. This means that a person's identity was determined by the group, clan, or family to which they belonged. Unlike our modern individualistic society, where everyone has an identity as unique, individual people, in Paul's day, a person did not have an identity in and of themselves but only through connection to a community.[1]

For example, a person's identity was partially based on their social class. A person's social class was determined

---

[1] David A. deSilva, *Honor, Patronage, Kinship & Purity: Unlocking New Testament Culture* (Downers Grove, IL: IVP Academic, 2000), 157–240.

by the family they were born into, with rare exceptions. There was also little room to climb the social ladder from the class into which you were born. For most people of the ancient world, their class identity was determined from birth and never changed.[2]

Thus for Paul to say that a follower of Jesus becomes a part of God's family is for him to say that their identity is now determined by Jesus. Their ethnicity or social class no longer determines who they are (e.g., there is no longer Jew and Greek or slave and free [Gal 3:28]). Their inheritance is no longer from their earthly father but from their heavenly Father. They live as members identified with God's family rather than a family of the world.

The second reason that this is significant is because family relationships are important. You do not choose your family. You are born into a family. Generally, but not always, family are the people who have always been and will always be there for you. So, for many, family bonds are the most important. Similarly, you do not choose the family of God. You are born, by baptism and the Spirit (Jn 3:5), into God's family. Therefore, for many, the bonds of God's family are some of the most important.

However, the age-old proverb says, "The blood of the covenant is thicker than the water of the womb,"[3] or the more popular, shorter version, "Blood is thicker than water."

---

[2] There was the possibility of social mobility. Social classes in the Greco-Roman world were not stagnant. However, upward movement was almost always initiated by someone higher in society sponsoring the lower individual. Watson, "Roman Social Classes."

[3] This proverb is of unknown origin.

There are a couple ways that this proverb can be understood. First, in popular thought, it is taken to mean that the bonds we choose to form are more powerful than the bonds we are born into. Unfortunately, not every family is a good family. The bonds within every family are not always good, and not every family has always and will always be there for each other. Therefore, many times, the bonds we choose to form with friends or our spouse are stronger than the bonds of our family.

However, it is believed that this proverb originally had a religious meaning. The bonds of the blood of Jesus in the new covenant (i.e., the bonds of the family of God) are, or at least should be, stronger than the bonds of the families we are born into. Jesus says in Luke 14:26, "Whoever comes to me and does not hate father and mother, wife and children, brothers and sisters, yes, and even life itself, cannot be my disciple." Jesus is saying that his followers are not meant merely to form a new family but something greater than a family, a family bonded by the blood he is preparing to shed.

However, I'm not sure that the church, in this lifetime, will ever fully achieve such family status. In mathematics, there is something called an asymptote. ChatGPT defines an asymptote in this way: "An asymptote is like a line that a curve gets closer and closer to, but never touches or crosses. It's as if they're forever reaching out to each other but never quite connecting." Family and church are like the curve and asymptote. The church should constantly be reaching toward the type of family life God desires of us, though we will never fully grasp it. However, this is not an excuse not to try!

If we are going to cultivate a culture that looks like the family of God, we must realize that relationships matter. Our bonds with one another matter, though relationships are not easy. People do things we don't like. They do things that annoy us and that we don't understand, or that we misunderstand. People even do things that harm us and damage us in some way. So, to maintain our family bonds, we must cultivate a culture of reconciliation.

Reconciliation in Colossians

Reconciliation speaks of unity, restoration, friendship, harmony, and peace. It is this kind of restoration, specifically in terms of the family of God, that Paul emphasizes in his interactions with the church in Colossae. The church in Colossae was primarily composed of Gentiles[4] and was one, like Rome, which Paul did not establish, but which was established because of Paul's evangelistic work.[5] The church was likely established by Epaphras, a coworker of Paul, during the time Paul was ministering in Ephesus (roughly 160 miles away).[6]

---

[4] Allan R. Bevere and John Frederick, "The Letter to the Colossians," in *Dictionary of Paul and His Letters: A Compendium of Contemporary Biblical Scholarship*, ed. Scot McKnight (Downers Grove, IL: IVP Academic, 2023), 141.

[5] Peter Thomas O'Brien, "The Letter to the Colossians," in *Dictionary of Paul and His Letters*, ed. Gerald F. Hawthorne, Ralph P. Martin, and Daniel G. Reid (Downers Grove, IL: InterVarsity Press, 1993), 147–48.

[6] Bevere and Frederick, "The Letter to the Colossians," 141.

We have two letters in the New Testament that Paul wrote to the church in Colossae— Colossians and Philemon. These letters were likely written and sent simultaneously,[7] possibly along with Ephesians, while Paul was in prison. If this is the case, Paul penned the letters sometime in the 50s.[8]

Both letters emphasize reconciliation—Colossians in a more theological way and Philemon more practically. In the opening chapter of Colossians, Paul says that through Jesus, the head of the church, "God was pleased to *reconcile* in himself all things, whether on earth or in heaven, by making *peace* through the blood of the cross" (Col 1:20). The Colossians, who were once "estranged," have, through Jesus, been "*reconciled* in his fleshly body through death, so as to present you holy and blameless and irreproachable before him" (Col 1:21–22).

Paul's words indicate that God is a God of reconciliation, which is rooted in God's act of creation, which Paul says was accomplished through Jesus (Col 1:16–17). One way to think of reconciliation is peace. When two people

---

[7] In Colossians 4:8–9, Paul says that Onesimus is coming, who is Philemon's slave, and the occasion for the letter to Philemon.

[8] As mentioned with Philippians, scholars debate the location of Paul's imprisonment. The traditional interpretation is Rome, but many recent scholars have suggested Ephesus. The location of Paul's imprisonment determines the dating of the letters, though Colossians must have been written before the devastating earthquake of 60-61 CE. Bevere and Frederick, "The Letter to the Colossians," 140–41; John Byron, "The Letter to Philemon," in *Dictionary of Paul and His Letters: A Compendium of Contemporary Biblical Scholarship*, ed. Scot McKnight (Downers Grove, IL: IVP Academic, 2023), 802.

have a dispute and reconcile, there is now peace in that relationship. For Jews, such as Paul, the idea of peace (in Hebrew, *shalom*) is that God created everything to have a place and proper function, and peace is when everything is in its proper place and functioning properly.[9] The original creation was the ideal of peace or reconciliation because everything had a place and was in its place. The birds were in the sky, sea creatures in the sea, animals on the dry ground, the sun in the day and moon in the evening, and human beings were ruling over God's creation as his image bearers. Therefore, God could declare his creation "good."

However, when sin entered God's creation, it stood in opposition to peace and reconciliation, bringing division and strife. Heaven, the place where God is, and earth, the place where we are, which were originally the same place, were divided. God tells Eve that there will be division between her and her husband, who will rule over her (Gn 3:16). He tells Adam that there will be strife between him and the ground, which will produce thorns and thistles (Gn 3:17–18). The second recorded sin is hostility within a family, as a brother kills a brother (Gn 4:1–16).

Paul says that God was pleased to reconcile heaven and earth through Jesus, thus bringing peace. Jesus, God come to tabernacle among us (Jn 1:14), is the bringing together of heaven and earth. Jesus's defeat of sin at the cross is the defeat of the division and strife that sin brings into the

---

[9] Drew Strait, "Peace, Reconciliation," in *Dictionary of Paul and His Letters: A Compendium of Contemporary Biblical Scholarship*, ed. Scot McKnight (Downers Grove, IL: IVP Academic, 2023), 792.

world, as all people are brought together in the family of God. Followers of Jesus, who are having their image-bearing ability restored, are able, through the power of the Spirit, to notice when things are not in their proper place or functioning properly, and to put things back in order. God is a God of reconciliation.

The reconciliation that God brings to his creation results in a new way of being human and interacting with one another. See Colossians 3:12–14:

> As God's chosen ones, holy and beloved, clothe yourselves with compassion, kindness, humility, meekness, and patience. Bear with one another and, if anyone has a complaint against another, forgive each other; just as the Lord has forgiven you, so you also must forgive. Above all, clothe yourselves with love, which binds everything together in perfect harmony.

Notice two things that Paul says. First, he says we are to "forgive each other" and connects this idea to "bear with one another." People are going to wrong and upset you; when they do, there are two ways to respond. You can give up, choose not to deal with it, stop interacting with them, and perhaps even move to a different church, or you can bear with them. You can stick it out, no matter how difficult or uncomfortable it makes you. For example, if you're married, I'm assuming when you're mad at your spouse, your first instinct is not to divorce them and move on to someone else; instead, you bear with them. The same must be true with our church family. We don't give up on family; we bear with them.

Here is my definition of forgiveness: forgiveness is no longer allowing a person's past actions to control your present and future. To forgive is to release the control that a person's past actions have over your life. When we fail to forgive someone, we are filled with anger, resentment, and jealousy, which control the way we talk to and treat that other person. To forgive is to release the control that those emotions have over us, and to allow our words and actions to be controlled by love.

Paul says that when we have a complaint against another, we forgive them. Notice that Paul says nothing about that person asking for or deserving forgiveness. Followers of Jesus recognize their faults and ask for forgiveness when they sin. They constantly pursue after Jesus, repenting and changing their actions when necessary. However, even when none of these occur, we must still forgive.

The reason is that Jesus has forgiven us. If we are truly followers of Jesus, we forgive as Jesus forgave. Jesus forgave us before we knew we needed forgiveness, before we asked for forgiveness, and before we did anything deserving of forgiveness. Despite our lack, Jesus still went to the cross to provide us forgiveness. Thus if we fail to forgive for any reason, we can rightly wonder whether we are following Jesus or something else.

Cultivating a church culture where we bear with and forgive each other begins with church leadership. Leaders must model this type of forgiveness. When someone talks badly about your sermon or program, how do you respond?

When a member begins gossiping about the leadership, how do you handle it? When people disagree with you, what do you do? Do you try to push them out of their position, or even worse, out of the church, or do you bear with them?

Perhaps the best way for a church to model such forgiveness is when a leader or minister sins. When a leader sins, they should be open, honest, and transparent with the church, especially those who were sinned against. State your wrongs and ask for forgiveness publicly. However, don't just cast the leader aside. Too often, when a church leader sins, they are fired or removed from their position, which forces them to find another church family. However, I'm not sure this is how a family should respond to one of their own. Instead, we bear with them, help them work through their moral failure, and forgive them for their wrong.

Now, there are two vital caveats. First, there are always exceptions to every rule. There are sins, such as child abuse, where figuring out how to bear with someone is more complicated. For legal and moral reasons, in these cases, everything cannot be forgiven, forgotten, and returned to normal. Second, a minister can commit sins that disqualify them from ministry. Forgiving and bearing with someone does not always mean they are restored to their previous position, but neither does it mean that they are tossed out to the curb to find a new family.

Paul also says that we should clothe ourselves with love because love "binds everything together in perfect harmony." Harmony is another word for peace or reconciliation. The church lives in harmony, with everyone filling the roles and functioning as God desires, when we love one another. Take some time to read 1 Corinthians 13:4–7 and note Paul's descriptions of love. If every member of the church lived out such love, how could there ever be division or hatred?

One final point needs to be made. Forgiveness, reconciliation, and bearing with one another are foundational to the church's life as a family. However, the church does not always operate in a way that allows these to occur. In churches where a leader or the leadership perpetuates abuse, it is still important to seek forgiveness and reconciliation and to bear with them. However, there comes a point where a person, for their own mental, physical, and spiritual health, cannot remain a part of that church. This is not an optimal situation, but if a leader or leadership is unwilling to repent of their wrong and harmful actions, there is sometimes no other alternative. I encourage the reader to consult Scot McKnight's book, *A Church Called Tov*,[10] where he discusses the issue of abuse in churches. McKnight does a tremendous job of balancing the need for forgiveness and reconciliation with the importance of protecting oneself from abusive leaders and finding healing.

It is also important to note that forgiveness does not always mean that we forget. If a leader is found stealing money, we can forgive them without allowing them to handle the money again. If a leader has been caught in abuse, we can forgive them without again putting people under their pastoral care. If a church is abusive, we can forgive without attending that church again. Just because we forgive does not

---

[10] McKnight, *A Church Called Tov.*

mean that we must needlessly put ourselves in harmful situations.

Reconciliation in Philemon

Colossians is Paul's theological approach to reconciliation. In Philemon, Paul puts this theology into practice. Philemon is Paul's shortest letter, just 335 Greek words, though the letter is powerful and has caused much scholarly debate. Philemon is a wealthy Gentile member of the church in Colossae. There has been some kind of dispute between Philemon and his slave, Onesimus, who has run away and encountered Paul. During his time with Paul, Onesimus was converted. Now, Paul is sending Onesimus back to his owner, Philemon, along with this letter imploring Philemon to accept Onesimus as a brother in Christ. And there are several things to point out.

Mediation

Onesimus has run away from his master, Philemon, but he might not be a runaway in the sense that would occur to a present-day American. Under certain Roman laws, slaves could seek an advocate or mediator when a dispute arose with their master.[11] Onesimus might not be a fugitive, running from both Philemon and the law, but rather seeking his right to an advocate by running to Paul, whom Onesimus likely knew from Philemon's interactions with Paul while Paul was ministering in Ephesus.

---

[11] Scot McKnight, *Pastor Paul: Nurturing a Culture of Christoformity in the Church* (Grand Rapids, MI: Brazos Press, 2019), 72.

If this or something similar is the case, it illustrates a significant point. Sometimes an advocate or mediator is needed to achieve reconciliation; sometimes a disagreement, or one side of a disagreement, becomes so heated and emotional that a third, neutral party is necessary. Now, Jesus says that when a problem arises, you are first to go to that person privately before gradually taking people with you (Mt 18:15–17). Jesus's words should be our first choice and ultimate desire. However, you no doubt know that sometimes going and speaking to someone alone is not the best idea. Perhaps you are too emotional and don't know what you might do or say. Perhaps the other person is too emotional, and your presence alone will only worsen matters. If a male leader is being inappropriate with a female member, she should not go and speak with him alone. In these cases, a mediator is needed.

This is important because sometimes, when a mediator is necessary, rather than finding one, we just don't deal with the problem. This is especially true among church leaders. Leaders seem to be embarrassed when they cannot handle disputes on their own, and rather than finding a mediator, they pretend that the problem doesn't exist. There is nothing wrong with seeking a mediator. It takes great maturity to realize that you cannot handle the situation yourself.

At other times, we seek a mediator when one isn't necessary. We just don't want to deal with the issue ourselves. I call this "church tattle-telling." Church tattle-telling is when someone wrongs you, and rather than making any effort to deal with the situation or speak to them, you run to an elder, minister, or another church leader. You tell that other person what happened and expect them to handle the issue. In your mind, you've done what you're supposed to do and don't have to worry about or deal with the situation any longer. However, that is not the case. The issue is not the responsibility of the elder or minister; it is your responsibility. The problem is still between you and that other person. Telling a leader does not get you out of your responsibility to bear with and forgive.

Church leaders would do well to resist the urge to facilitate church tattle-telling. Don't get involved when someone comes to you with a problem between them and another person and there is no reason for you to be involved. Tell them you are always here to help and will be a mediator if necessary, but for now, the two of them need to try and work through the problem themselves.

The Whole Church

Though primarily addressed to Philemon, this letter was meant to be read before the whole church. In verse 2, Paul addresses the letter to "the church in your house." Sibling disputes within God's family are whole church matters.

Our individualistic society says that my business is none of your business. If I have a problem with so-and-so, it is between me and them; it doesn't concern you. However, Paul would disagree. My problem with you or your problem with me is a concern for the whole church because it impacts the health of the whole church. A church is only as healthy as the members who make it up.

This is not a license to gossip about others or stick your nose into deeply private business. Some things take place in a church, elders meeting, or counseling session that must remain private, even within a family. However, what this does mean is that people have a right to seek advice from one family member when dealing with another. It is perfectly fine to go to someone wiser and more experienced than yourself and ask for advice on dealing with a problem or to seek someone out as a mediator.

It also means that each member has a responsibility to facilitate reconciliation. If you see a problem not being dealt with, you are responsible for encouraging people to reconcile. If people need a mediator, you are responsible for being a mediator. The most important responsibility you have is to pray for reconciliation.

At this point, talking about another church phenomenon is necessary: righteous gossip. Sometimes, when there is a problem between two people, and we know what's going on, we run and tell the elders, minister, or other leader. We believe we're doing the right thing because we know that an unresolved issue plagues the whole church, and thus we're telling the people who need to know. We feel righteous for doing so, but in fact we're merely gossiping.

There are times when leadership needs to know about an unresolved issue. A leader likely needs to be informed when a problem goes on for an extended time, spreads to other members, or seems to have stopped moving toward a resolution. However, if it is a minor or mediocre issue in the process of being resolved, there is no need to gossip about it, even to a church leader.

Leaders would do well to fight the urge to facilitate righteous gossiping. If someone tells you something you don't need to know, politely tell them that it is information that does not need to be shared. Let them know that you're here if the issue gets worse or hits a stalemate, but it is not something that currently needs your attention.

Compulsion

Paul's ultimate wish is to keep Onesimus with him to help his work for the Gospel, but he won't do so without Philemon's approval. In verses 13–14, Paul says:

> I wanted to keep him with me, so that he might be of service to me in your place during my imprisonment for the gospel; but I preferred to do nothing without your consent, in order that your good deed might be voluntary and not something forced.

Reconciliation cannot be by compulsion; it must be voluntary. You cannot force two people to reconcile. If someone is mad at you, you cannot force them to forgive you.

The only person you can control is yourself. In Peter Steinke's book *Congregational Leadership in Anxious Times*, he discusses the importance of church leaders being a "non-anxious presence." When problems arise in a congregation, so does individuals' anxiety. A healthy leader does not respond to anxiety with more anxiety but seeks to curb the anxious feelings by being a non-anxious presence. Steinke says that a leader can be a non-anxious presence by knowing their limits and the limits of others, having clarity about what they believe, taking stands with courage, staying the course, and staying connected to others.[12]

Everything Steinke says can be summarized by saying that when problems arise, you must realize that you can only control yourself. You cannot control what others think, say, or do, but you can control how you respond. You respond to anger by admitting your faults. You respond to hate with love. You respond to resentment with forgiveness. You might not be able to control others or the final outcome, but you can allow yourself to be controlled by the fruit of the Spirit. And most importantly, when the situation is entirely out of your control, you can pray. You can turn the problem over to God and allow God to lead people to reconciliation.

However, just because you cannot force people to reconcile does not mean you can allow a lack of reconciliation to establish deep, harmful roots in your congregation. As mentioned earlier, the health of the individuals and their relationships in the church impacts the health of the entire church. When two people are at odds, and they gossip about each other, it hurts the whole church. When people try to make others take sides, it hurts the entire church. When members are unable to be in the same room or work together to pursue God's mission, it hurts the entire church.

This is where leaders must take a stand with courage. They must have the courage to say, "We cannot force you to do anything, but we can keep you from taking the entire

---

[12] Peter L. Steinke, "Congregational Leadership in Anxious Times: Being Calm and Courageous No Matter What" (Lanham, MD: Rowman & Littlefield, 2006).

church down with you." Hard lines may need to be drawn. Leaders may need to say that while two people don't have to be friends now, they cannot bring the church into their dispute. Leaders may even need to take a stand, as Jesus instructs in Matthew 18:15–17, and say that a person can either stop gossiping and spreading division or they need to leave the church.

Don't Forget the Past

When you read through Philemon, you'll quickly notice the deep, intimate relationship that Paul has with Philemon. Thus much of Paul's plea is built upon their history, relationship, and love for each other. Paul says in verse 7, "I have indeed received much joy and encouragement from your love, because the hearts of the saints have been refreshed through you, my brother," and in verse 19, "I, Paul, am writing with my own hand: I will repay it. I say nothing about your owing me even your own self."

One problem when disagreements arise is that it is easy to get so caught up in the present problem that we forget our past relationship with the other person. Too often, two people who have been through thick and thin and who have done tremendous good for each other (and for others) lose their relationship over one disagreement. This happens because they get so caught up in the present problem that they forget about the strength of their relationship throughout the past.

So, for reconciliation to occur, we must deal with the present problem but in a way that does not forget about the good relationship we have had in the past. The person we have the problem with isn't a bad person; perhaps they've done something bad or made a mistake, but our past experiences with them witness to the fact that they are not a bad person. We don't hate them; on the contrary, our past shows just how deeply we love them. We might not see eye to eye now, but our past demonstrates that we can do great good together. These reminders of the past must govern our interactions in the present.

Conclusion

Ultimately, we must never forget that the church is a family, and families have disputes. It's inevitable. The question is not whether we will have disputes but how we will handle them. Will we handle disputes like the family of God, or as the world does? Will we approach disputes as servants of a God of reconciliation, who forgave us even before we recognized our need for forgiveness? Will we seek a mediator only when necessary, recognize that our disputes impact the health of the whole church, resist the urge to force reconciliation by only controlling ourselves, and never forget the past?

8

Thessalonica
A Culture of Hope

If you could find out the exact day and time you will die, would you want to know? That's a challenging question, and I'm not sure there is a right or wrong answer. Some might say they don't want to know because they fear becoming complacent if they discover they will live for a long time. If they find out they'll live for another hundred years, they might put important things off until the end. Others might say they want to know so they can take full advantage of every moment. If they discover they will only live for another year, they want to take advantage of every moment for the next 365 days.

Perhaps an easier question might be, would you want to know future events in the short term? Would you want to know where you're going? What your career will look like? When you'll retire? When you'll become a grandparent?

There is likely something in your future that you would love to know. Perhaps it is something just mentioned, or maybe it's a problem you're currently dealing with. A situation at your job, in your family, or with a friend that you're anxious about because you don't know how it will turn out.

So, you want to know the future, how things will end, and whether everything will work out.

Our desire to know things about the future is often due to anxiety. Some have more anxiety than others, but we all, from time to time, battle anxious feelings. Google defines anxiety as follows: "a feeling of worry, nervousness, or unease, typically about an imminent event or something with an uncertain outcome." And there are different types of anxiety. Sometimes we get anxious because of one of the bad situations previously mentioned. Some people have social anxiety, and the unknown of social situations makes them anxious. Then, there is a level of anxiety that is diagnosable, when anxiety begins to negatively impact personal well-being and keeps an individual from doing the things they want or need.

I believe that normal anxiety, not the diagnosable psychological condition, is often because of our human desire for hope. If you've spent much time in church, you've probably heard a definition of "biblical hope" that goes something like this: Hope is not wishful thinking; it is an assurance of the future. This is not a terrible definition. When the Bible talks about hope, it is not talking about merely wishing that this or that will happen, but it is talking about knowing, with certainty, that something will happen in the future. However, there is more to the story.

Biblical hope is the assurance of what the future will hold, how events will turn out, and what the ending of our and the world's story will be. Hope is the relief of some of our anxiety because we know the conclusion. Though hope is not merely future-oriented, it changes how we live now because we know what our actions and lives are working towards.

However, I believe that only followers of Jesus possess this kind of hope. As Jesus followers, we know that the God of the universe, who is fully in control, and who revealed himself in Jesus of Nazareth, has told us what the future holds and how the world's story will end. The rest of the world does not have such knowledge. As a result, they seem to be living in hopelessness. Consider what someone who is not a follower of Jesus must see when they look out into the world.

They see income inequalities as the gap between the wealthy and poor continues to widen. They see mental health issues as rates of depression and anxiety grow, particularly among young people. They see environmental degradation as pollution and deforestation plague our planet. They see social polarization as division along political, social, and cultural lines deepen. They see poverty and hunger as millions of people worldwide lack access to basic necessities.

When someone who does not follow Jesus looks out into the world, the brokenness they see seems hopeless, but not so with the church, for the church cultivates a culture of hope.

Hope in Thessalonica

When Paul writes his two letters to the Thessalonians, he deals heavily with questions about the future and how the world's story will end. Paul, Silas, and Timothy, the authors of 1 and 2 Thessalonians, established the church in Thessalonica during Paul's first missionary journey. These two letters are also likely the first Paul ever wrote, with 1 Thessalonians dating to around 50 CE.[1]

The Thessalonians are suffering as they deal with persecution. They also have questions about the future. They want to know what tomorrow is going to hold and when their suffering is going to end. Specifically, Paul addresses three questions: What happens to people who die before Christ returns? When will Christ return? Have we already missed Christ's return?

Paul responds to the Thessalonians' suffering and questions by reminding them of the hope they have in Jesus, which he taught them during his time in Thessalonica. They have hope that the evil of the world will not get the final say. Paul says that those who are causing their suffering have been "constantly … filling up the measure of their sins; but God's wrath has overtaken them at last" (1 Thes 2:16), that God will "repay with affliction those who afflict you" (2 Thes 1:6), and that when Jesus returns he will inflict "vengeance on those who do not know God and on those who do not obey the gospel of our Lord Jesus" (2 Thes 1:8).

The Thessalonians might be suffering as evil seems to be winning, but this will not be the case forever. Eventually, God will judge and destroy the evil and sin of the world. The kingdom of God will win the victory, and a new heaven and new earth will be created.

---

[1] F. F. Bruce, *1 & 2 Thessalonians*, Word Biblical Commentary 45 (Waco, TX: Word Books, 1982), xxxiv–xxxvi; Gordon D. Fee and Douglas Stuart, *How to Read the Bible Book by Book: A Guided Tour* (Grand Rapids, MI: Zondervan, 2002), 364.

Not only will God one day fully defeat the powers of evil, but in doing so, he will rescue the Thessalonians, as followers of Jesus, to the new creation. Paul says that Jesus "rescues us from the wrath that is coming" (1 Thes 1:10), has "destined us not for wrath but for obtaining salvation" (1 Thes 5:9), and that they will "obtain the glory of our Lord Jesus Christ" (2 Thes 2:14).

Since the Thessalonians have such a hope, they can know, with complete assurance, that God will defeat the powers of evil and rescue them to the new creation. Thus Paul says that they are not to grieve as those who do not possess this hope. 1 Thessalonians 4:13–18 reads:

> But we do not want you to be uninformed, brothers and sisters, about those who have died, so that you may not grieve as others do who have no hope. For since we believe that Jesus died and rose again, even so, through Jesus, God will bring with him those who have died. For this we declare to you by the word of the Lord, that we who are alive, who are left until the coming of the Lord, will by no means precede those who have died. For the Lord himself, with a cry of command, with the archangel's call and with the sound of God's trumpet, will descend from heaven, and the dead in Christ will rise first. Then we who are alive, who are left, will be caught up in the clouds together with them to meet the Lord in the air; and so we will be with the Lord forever. Therefore encourage one another with these words.

The world might be filled with death and sadness, but the Thessalonians have hope. They grieve when they lose someone whom they have loved, but they grieve with the hope of resurrection. The hope that one day, all will be raised to live eternally in the new creation.

The Church's Culture of Hope

So, how do we cultivate a culture of hope in our churches?

Future-Oriented

First, we live in a future-oriented way. In earlier chapters, we briefly discussed new creation theology—where we are going is where we have come from. Heaven will be God's creation of a new heaven and a new earth—a return to Eden. The new heaven and new earth will be a creation that functions in the way God originally created and designed it.

Our knowledge of where we are going is important because it determines how we live now. As followers of Jesus, we have decided to become active characters in God's story. Everyone lives based on the story or narrative they tell themselves. These stories are powerful and are typically stories that have developed since childhood.

In *Atomic Habits*, James Clear discusses the power that small changes in habits can have in completely transforming our lives. In the book, he emphasizes that the easiest and best way to develop habits is through identity. Our identity, who we believe ourselves to be and the stories we tell ourselves, are the strongest motivators for changing our behavior.[2] If you constantly tell yourself that you are bad at math, if that is the story you live in, then you will probably always be bad at math. However, if you choose to develop a story where you believe yourself to be a musician, then learning how to play the violin will be much easier.

We all live as characters in some story. As followers of Jesus, our story is God's story. God's story is a story that moves from creation to new creation in light of the cross. We live now as active characters in a story that is moving towards new creation. Thus when we look out into the world and see seemingly hopeless evil, we respond with hope. As active characters in God's story, we work to redeem God's creation, wipe out evil when we see it, and bring heaven to earth. We live out Jesus's prayer, "Your kingdom come. Your will be done, on earth as it is in heaven" (Mt 6:10).

A response of hope does not sit around and do nothing about evil because one day God will take care of it. This is the response of too many churches, and it is not a response of hope but of hopelessness. Yes, one day, God will solve the problem of evil, but if that hope has no legs to stand on in the present, then it does nothing to provide us with hope now. We are still left alone to figure out how to deal with our real-life hopeless situations. A hopeful response does not say that the church should not speak to the issues in our world, should not get involved in political questions, or should not engage non-believers because that's God's job.

Instead, a hopeful response participates in God's current activity to redeem his creation. God is already at work

---

[2] Clear, *Atomic Habits.*

to redeem the world. Christians are not deists; we don't believe that God got the world running and now sits back observing from a distance. On the contrary, we firmly believe that God is actively working in the world. The conclusion of God's activity is a new heaven and a new earth, and God will accomplish this by his power and sovereignty alone. God does not need our help.

While God does not need our help, he is glad to display his power through our broken, earthly vessels (2 Cor 4:7). God doesn't need us, but when we know where the story is going, how can we not desire to participate in what God is already doing? So we live in a way that seeks to put the world back together. When people are hungry, we feed them (see Jas 2:15–16). When evil occurs, we call it evil. When politicians, regardless of political party, do things that help the disadvantaged, we celebrate. When they create policies that are harmful or dangerous, we stand opposed.

Now, there is an important caveat. The job of the church is not to rule the country. The church is not a theocracy, nor does God primarily display his power through powerful people and institutions. As shown in the cross, God's power is displayed through weakness (see chapter 3) and the church (see chapter 5). The church doesn't seek power to rule or force non-Christians to live like Christians; the church simply lives and works as people of hope by redeeming creation in the spaces and places we work and live, no matter how big or small.

A hopeful response also proclaims hope to the hopeless. People who are caught up in the evil and brokenness of the world lack hope, but we know there is hope found in

Jesus—the hope of the cross that one day evil will be destroyed. The church provides hope in a hopeless world, not merely by seeking to overcome evil, but also by giving people the hope of the Gospel.

When people walk into your church every week, members and visitors alike are searching for hope. They honestly don't care about many of the things those of us who are ministers or church leaders care about. They don't care about the intricate nature of the Trinity. They don't care about the church budget. They care about putting food on the table. They care about the upcoming election. They are concerned about the meaninglessness of their dead-end job.

It's not wrong to talk about the Trinity or the budget, but how often does your church give people hope? How many sermons are sermons of hope? What kind of services does your church offer to give people hope (e.g., counseling services, food pantry)?

Finally, cultivating a culture of hope means that when we find ourselves caught up in the hopelessness of evil, we remember that God is working behind the scenes, even when we cannot see him. Evil might seem to control our lives now, but God is truly in control. He will win the victory; evil will not get the final say. Our congregations need to hear this message every time they enter our doors. It is so easy to get caught up in the hopelessness of our world and forget that God is in control. There might be many good things we desire for people to know about God, and we need to teach those as well, but at a bare minimum, every week, people should leave our services with a renewed hope that God is at work in the world and their lives.

Grieve with Hope

Second, a culture of hope grieves with hope. When Paul speaks to the Thessalonians about grief, he does not say that they should not grieve. The death of a loved one, especially an untimely death, is a tragic event whether you're a Christian or not. So, as Christians, we still grieve our loss, but we do not grieve as non-Christians who have no hope. We grieve with the knowledge that we will get to see our loved ones again. We grieve knowing that death does not get the final say. We grieve with the hope of new creation.

When someone has experienced a loss, it is not the time to provide theological reflection about death and grief. When people are grieving, they do not need our theology; they need our presence. However, how we present ourselves can either accentuate or damage our proclamation of hope. Do we present ourselves in a way that says this is the end, or that there's hope in the future? How do we speak at funerals? Do we provide hope for the new creation?

Live Outside the Powers

Finally, a culture of hope lives outside the powers. Our world has particular methods of operation. The world moves forward based on three things: money, intelligence, and elected officials. Our world thinks any problem can be solved with more money, intelligence, or the correct elected official. However, in practice, none of these seem to have any impact on our broken world. No matter how much money we have, how intelligent we are, or who is elected to a particular office, the world keeps spinning in a hopeless fashion. There is still violence and poverty, regardless.

We have discussed this in previous chapters, but sometimes, the church's response to evil is to try and solve it through worldly means. We think if we just had more money, if we could just come up with the right solution, or if we elect the correct official, then the problems would be solved. However, when we do, and the problems still exist, rather than giving us hope, it makes us feel even more hopeless. When we place our hope in the wrong thing and it fails to come through, we're left wondering if there is anything that will solve our hopelessness.

So, as churches of hope, we live outside the powers of the world. We don't solve the world's problems with money, intelligence, or elected officials but with the hope of the Gospel. We solve them by relying on the power of God through the Holy Spirit, which is already in the process of redeeming the creation and will finally redeem all things when Christ returns.

Such a hope reveals itself in the church's problem-solving response. As long as we live in this world, the church will require money. So, when we want to build a new building, increase our giving to the poor, or create a community activity, we must raise money. The question isn't, should we raise money, but how do we go about raising money? What do our words and actions say about where we place our hope? Is our hope in the money or God?

When we raise money, we do so not because we believe the money will solve our problem but because we believe God has called us as a church to do something that takes money to accomplish. God is the active agent, not our money. We step forward in faith by beginning what we believe God has called us to, knowing that if it is God's will, he will provide the funding. When we fail to get enough money, we don't see it as a defeat but perhaps as God calling us in a different direction.

When a problem arises, we begin the process of discerning a solution with prayer. We take days, weeks, and months to pray before proposing solutions, brainstorming, or putting together committees. Our churches move into the future by placing their faith in God's guidance, not our intellectual ability to develop appropriate solutions.

We don't look to elected officials to solve the world's problems. Never should it be said in the pulpit of Christ's church that if so-and-so is elected, it will solve the evil of our country, nor that if so-and-so is elected, the future of our country is hopeless. Our future is never hopeless if we rely on God's power. Our churches must engage our world by talking about political issues (e.g., abortion, LGBTQ rights, poverty), but we do so not through the lens of partisan politics but through the cross. We don't put our hope in elected officials but in the power of God that is already at work in the world, in God's ability to work his power through our broken, earthly vessels through our choice to be active participants in God's story that is moving toward a new creation.

Conclusion

The best examples of living with hope in God's new creation are the stories of early Christian martyrs and the monastic tradition. If you read the writings of early Christian martyrs, a consistent theme is their focus on God's future.

They were able to stand firm and were willing to lose their lives for their faith because they knew that this world was not their home and that one day, God will resurrect their bodies to live in the new creation. Such resolve is only possible through the hope of Jesus Christ.

Most scholars believe that the lives of early Christian martyrs led to the development of monasticism. Once Constantine converted to Christianity in 312 and Christianity became the religion of the empire, the faith and hope present in the early martyrs had to take a new form. No longer was hope defined by faithfulness in the face of persecution and death. This led to the establishment of monasteries, where monks would forsake the pleasures of the world (e.g., money, marriage, etc.) to live in service to God through constant prayer, study, and religious community.

Imagine the type of hope in God's future it takes to give up your life or reject money and marriage. Such hope is a hope that most Christians, and probably the majority of Americans, do not possess. We tend to be now-oriented rather than heaven-oriented. However, the hope found in Jesus and the examples of early Christian martyrs and monastics provide us with a picture that counters the concerns of this world and focuses on God's promise of a new creation.

9

The Pastoral Epistles
A Culture of Godly Leadership

The final Pauline letter I want to consider is actually a series of letters referred to as the Pastoral Epistles.[1] The Pastoral Epistles include 1 and 2 Timothy and Titus. These letters are called 'pastoral' because they deal with pastoral advice and qualifications that Paul is providing to Timothy, a leader in the church in Ephesus, and Titus, a leader in the church in Crete.[2] There is a massive amount of scholarly

---

[1] The Pastoral Epistles are the most heavily debated letters in the New Testament that bear Paul's name. Most scholars do not believe Paul wrote the letters, and many date them into the second century, after Paul's lifetime. Regardless, most scholars see a connection between the three letters or believe they were all composed by the same author. The purpose of this book is not to delve into questions of authorship but to recognize the inspiration of all the books of our New Testament and their benefit for cultivating church cultures. L. M. Kidson, "Pastoral Epistles," in *Dictionary of Paul and His Letters: A Compendium of Contemporary Biblical Scholarship*, ed. Scot McKnight (Downers Grove, IL: IVP Academic, 2023), 757–58.

[2] The reference to these letters as "pastoral" dates back to Thomas Aquinas (1274), who, in his commentary on 1 Timothy, said it was "like a pastoral rule." The modern term comes from Paul Anton,

debate about the authorship, date, and recipients of these letters. Since this is the case, we will not spend time trying to ascertain the background of the letters but take them at face value for what they might contribute to our conversation about cultivating church cultures.

Selecting and Installing Leaders

The Pastoral Epistles might be most well-known and used for their qualifications of elders (1 Tm 3:1–7; Ti 1:5–9) and deacons (1 Tm 3:8–13). Ever since these words were penned, churches have looked to these passages when selecting and installing leaders. Though the Pastoral Epistles contain a plethora of additional information that is helpful for church cultures, it is vital that we understand the significance of selecting and installing leaders.

The Importance of the Leadership Selection Process

Selecting and installing church leaders might be the most important process for a church to establish a good, Spirit-powered church culture. As mentioned throughout this book, church leaders play a pivotal role in all aspects of cultivating church culture. While church members also play

---

who, in lectures dating from 1726–27, said that several New Testament letters are pastoral and useful for ministry, though he referred to the letters to Timothy and Titus as *pastoral Scripta par excellence*. These letters do contain teachings regarding leaders and leadership selection, but not exclusively so. Additionally, all of the Bible could rightly be called 'pastoral,' as it all helps to shepherd God's people and cultivate shepherds in our churches. So, while the name Pastoral Epistles is a correct definition, it is not all-inclusive. Kidson, 756–57.

an essential role and can significantly influence a church's culture, I am not convinced that good membership can overcome poor leadership. For a church to have a culture that propels it into the future as an active participant in God's story, it must have healthy leadership.

However, the specific individuals appointed as leaders are not the only aspect of selecting church leaders that impacts a church's culture. So does the actual process of selecting leaders. Doug Peters, my preaching and ministry professor at Oklahoma Christian University, says that leader function is determined by leadership selection. The way leaders are chosen determines how leaders function, and their function is what helps to cultivate the church's culture.

Church leaders are chosen from two places—within the church and outside the church. In churches with elders and deacons, these roles are generally filled by people within the church. The other leadership roles, typically various minister or pastor positions, are generally filled by people outside the church through appointment or an interview process.

The ways that the people who fill these positions are chosen are as varied as the number of churches that exist, but nevertheless, have a drastic impact on a church's culture. For example, if elders are chosen through a democratic process that resembles the American political election, with elders "campaigning" and a majority rules vote, we should not be surprised when an eldership functions like politicians. If a minister is chosen primarily because of their speaking ability, then we should expect them to function as a good speaker but not necessarily as a good minister to the congregants.

Many times, poor leadership is the result of a poor leadership selection process. The process of selecting and installing leaders is just as important as the qualities of the leaders being appointed. This is why Paul says, "Do not ordain anyone hastily" (1 Tm 5:22a). With that being said, it is crucial for us to consider the "qualifications" of church leaders.

Qualifications vs. Qualities

Most modern Bibles have a heading over the passages in 1 Timothy and Titus that speak about elders and deacons, identifying the sections as "qualifications" for these offices. However, qualifications are a poor way to understand these passages. Qualifications signify that a person must perfectly meet each of the stated qualifications, and if they do, they can hold the particular office. There are numerous problems with this approach, but I want to name just three.

First, it produces the mindset that every leader will be perfectly skilled in every qualification, though we know this is unrealistic. A leader might be perfect at self-control but, while displaying hospitality, may still have room to grow and mature in this area. This is not to say that we should appoint a leader with a drastic shortcoming in a particular area, but neither should we disqualify someone who still has room to grow. If that were the case, we could never appoint leaders.

Second, qualifications make us think that if a person meets all of them, then they can automatically be appointed. The problem is that a person can have all the "qualifications" but not be the right leader for a particular church at a particular time. The needs of a church differ based on the church's location and makeup and change over time as the church and community change. This is why we talked about the importance of casting a vision that includes the past, present, and future. The same is true regarding church leadership. The type of leader a church needs depends on the church's location and makeup. A good leader at one church will not necessarily be the right leader at another church, though they both may meet all the qualifications. A church must consider its particular needs and the type of person that its congregation will follow, in addition to the qualifications listed by Paul. In the end, a person can meet all the qualifications, but if it is not the man that Christ wants to lead his church, or it is not a man the church is willing to follow, then their qualifications are a moot point.[3] Christ calls specific people at specific times to lead his church into the future.

Third, qualifications force us to create a final, black-and-white list of qualifications. The problem is that many of the qualifications are not black and white. What does it mean to be the husband of one wife (in Greek, it is literally "a one-woman man")? How much wine is too much? Are the women mentioned in 1 Timothy 3:11 the wives of the deacons or female deacons? These questions don't even mention the fact that the lists for elders in 1 Timothy and Titus contain different qualifications. Different churches are going to answer these questions differently. The problem is that if we see the lists as qualifications, there is no room for different interpretations.

---

[3] Dave Bland, "Background, Qualities, and Function of Elders in the Church," *Journal of Christian Studies* 2, no. 3 (September 2023): 23–40.

Therefore, I would propose interpreting these lists as qualities rather than qualifications. The lists contain qualities of being a good leader, but a particular church might need people who have additional qualities to be good leaders for that church. Every leader should display these qualities, but they may be stronger in one than another. Qualities allow for different interpretations of some of the more difficult points of the list. For example, the quality of a man who is the husband of one wife speaks to his faithfulness and treatment of his wife rather than to whether he has been divorced.[4] Not being addicted to too much wine does not speak of a particular amount a leader is allowed to consume but of the quality of not being addicted to anything that might hinder a person's ability to lead.

How Should Leaders Be Selected?

In light of the above discussion, how should church leaders be selected? They should be selected through a process of spiritual discernment.[5] A spiritually discerning selection process looks to the Holy Spirit as the guide for who will be selected. It is not a majority rule or the selection of the most popular person, but it is finding and appointing the people God has called and gifted to fill the roles and needs of a particular localized church congregation.

A process of spiritual discernment begins with prayer and fasting. A selection process that does not begin with time with God and allowing God to enter into the process

---

[4] Bland.

[5] This language is borrowed from Doug Peters.

will be a process that selects leaders based on worldly standards rather than the people God has called and gifted to fill the role. So, a Spirit-filled church culture will always begin selecting leaders through spending time with the Spirit.

The next step in the process is to ask the right question. The question should not be who is the most popular. Who has succeeded in the business world? Who meets every qualification? Who is the best public speaker? Rather, the question should be, who has been called and gifted by God to lead this congregation at this time in our effort to be active participants in God's story?

The actual process of selecting an individual can go in a multitude of ways. I do not believe any way is right or wrong, though perhaps some ways are better attuned to facilitating a process of spiritual discernment. However, here is what I have found to be the most effective. I believe you should always include the congregation in the discernment process. The Spirit works in different ways in different people who come from different backgrounds, have different experiences, and are a part of different generations. Therefore, the process should include the discernment of the Spirit in the lives of these different people. Also, allowing the congregation to participate in the selection will help the transition process because the congregation can take ownership in the selection of the new leader. This can be done through church voting, submitting names, or a committee comprising a multi-generational cross-section of the church.[6]

---

[6] If a committee is used, it should reflect the church's demographics. The committee should be intergenerational and made up

However, the selection process should not be purely democratic. Nowhere in the Bible do we have an example of decisions among God's people being made by a majority rules vote. The church's affinity for a democratic process is influenced by American democracy rather than Scripture. Therefore, while it is vital to incorporate the congregation in the process, the ultimate decision lies in the church's leadership, which God has appointed to guide and direct the congregation.

Therefore, I believe it is best to allow a congregation to submit names or a committee to interview and submit a recommendation to the church leadership (i.e., board, elders, or however your leadership is structured). The leaders can then spend time in discussion, prayer, and discernment before accepting the recommendation(s) made by the congregation or committee.

Such a process helps to prevent a couple of common problems when churches select leaders. First, by not following a purely democratic process, the church prevents itself from selecting the most popular person rather than the one called by God to lead. It also prevents one group of the church from having too much influence in the decision. For example, many smaller churches have one or two families that comprise most of the membership. If a purely democratic process occurred, those families would choose the leaders, and the other families' opinions would be left out.

---

of multiple genders and people with different experiences, as is reflected in the congregation at large.

Second, including the church prevents the current leadership from selecting people they want rather than the people God believes the church needs. For example, it is easy for the current leadership to select people who believe the same things they do, but God might desire to add a diversity of opinions to the church's leadership. Leaderships can also be tempted to select their friends or family members to try and increase their power and influence in the church. Not allowing the current leaders to choose the new leaders solely prevents a power grab from taking place.

The Role of Church Leaders

There have been entire books written on the role of leaders, ministers, and elders.[7] The purpose of this book is not to fully define any of these leadership positions. However, how leaders understand and perform their roles impacts a church's culture. Therefore, I believe there are a few brief but vital points to be made about the roles of these leadership positions.

---

[7] Some books that I recommend for church leaders include: Thomas G. Long, *The Witness of Preaching*, Second Edition (Louisville, KY: Westminster John Knox Press, 2005); McKnight, *Pastor Paul: Nurturing a Culture of Christoformity in the Church*; Thomas C. Oden, *Classical Pastoral Care*, vols. 1–4 (New York: Crossroad, 1987); Tim Sensing (ed.), *The Effective Practice of Ministry* (Abilene, TX: Abilene Christian University Press, 2013); and William H. Willimon, *Pastor: The Theology and Practice of Ordained Ministry* (Nashville, TN: Abingdon Press, 2002).

The Role of Elders

In 1 Timothy 3:1–7 and Titus 1:5–9, Paul gives the qualities for church elders. In 1 Timothy, the term Paul uses for elders is overseer or bishop (gk. *episkopos*). In Titus, Paul also uses the Greek word for overseer but adds the term translated as "elder" (gk. *presbyterous*), a word that refers to an older person.

Overseer refers to an elder's administration, delegation, and decision-making role.[8] However, this administrative role is spiritual. It refers to overseeing the church's spiritual life, the spiritual health of church members, and directing the church into the future as an active participant in God's story. For this reason, the New Testament uses the imagery of an elder as a shepherd or pastor (gk. *poimēn*). An elder is to guide, direct, and protect the church as a shepherd does his sheep.

Since this is a spiritual responsibility, an elder's primary job is to deal with spiritual matters, not matters relating to finances, staff, outreach, programs, or building maintenance. These are jobs that must be delegated to others. A finance committee can oversee the church's money and spending. A lead minister should oversee, hire, and fire church staff. A deacon can oversee church building maintenance. By delegating these responsibilities, the elders are freed to deal with the church's spiritual needs. This principle is seen in Acts 6:1–6 when the apostles appoint men to care

---

[8] Bland, "Background, Qualities, and Function of Elders in the Church," 35.

for the neglected widows because they realize they have other and more important matters to attend to.[9]

This does not mean that an elder does not have any responsibility in these other matters. Part of leading and guiding a church means ensuring all aspects of a church's life are being faithfully stewarded and are aiding the church's desire to participate in God's story. However, their primary responsibility and the majority of their time and energy should be given to spiritual matters.

Finally, Paul refers to elders as older people. An older person as a leader and decision-maker likely dates back to the elders at the city gates in the Old Testament. The older men of a city, who were believed to be wise, would gather at the city gate to make decisions for the city. These gate meetings developed into legislative groups in Israel and, eventually, the Sanhedrin, though the tie is not direct. This is likely the tradition to which Paul is appealing when speaking about church leaders as older people who are wise and mature in the faith and capable of guiding and making decisions for the church.[10]

The Role of Deacon

The text of 1 Timothy 3:8–13 lists qualities for deacons (gk. *diakonos*). The term deacon refers to a table servant. The noun and verb form are used by Jesus at the Last Supper when instructing his disciples to lead by serving, "But not so

---

[9] In this passage, the verb form of the Greek word for deacon is used.

[10] Bland, "Background, Qualities, and Function of Elders in the Church," 24–26.

with you; rather the greatest among you must become like the youngest, and the leader like one who *serves*. For who is greater, the one who is at the table or the one who *serves*? Is it not the one at the table? But I am among you as one who *serves*" (Lk 22:26–27). The verb form is also used of the men appointed by the apostles to wait on the tables of the widows who were missing out on the daily distribution of food (Acts 6:2).

The sole role of a deacon is to be a servant. They serve the church in areas that need to be done to help the church be an active participant in God's story. They are not primarily leaders. For the church to be effective and efficient in participating in God's mission, many things need to get done. The church building needs to be maintained. A budget needs to be created, and spending needs to be monitored. Video and audio equipment, the church website, and social media must be managed. These are vital to a church's future, vision, and culture.

The great news is that God always provides the people and gifts a church needs to participate in his story. Therefore, a person is not appointed a deacon because they are a good person, and then the church needs to find a way to use them; a deacon is not appointed, and then the church finds something for them to do. A deacon is appointed because they are filled with the Holy Spirit and have been gifted by God to fill a real need in the church's life that impacts its ability to participate in God's story. Deacons are appointed to serve the church and the mission of God.

Therefore, the process of appointing a deacon might look something like this. The church needs someone to take over its website and social media. A member of the congregation has shown interest in the technical and digital aspects of the church's life and has proven to be gifted in their use. Another member notices this member's gifts, willingness, and the fact that they have already been serving in this area in an unofficial capacity. They then recommend this person to the current leadership as a possible deacon. The leadership takes time to pray for the Spirit's guidance and speak to this member. Once the leaders and the member feel that the Spirit is leading them in this direction, the member is publicly appointed a deacon.

The Role of the Minister/Pastor

All leadership roles are essential for the development of a church's culture. However, the role of minister could, debatably, be the most important. The minister is the face of the congregation. The one who speaks the word of God to the congregation each week. The person people come to with their problems and struggles. The one who greets and interacts with visitors. Therefore, the minister might be the most influential single person in the cultivation of a church's culture.

The minister is typically the member with the most theological, biblical, and ministerial training and sometimes the only member with such training. This reality cannot be overlooked. I believe it is vital for a church to have a leadership structure that places the church in the hands of multiple people. If a single minister is the ultimate leader, it opens the church to the real possibility of abuse of leadership. Though a multiplicity of leaders is important, the education and experience of a trained minister cannot be overlooked and should be heavily considered during any minister selection process.

The church needs people trained and educated in interpreting the Bible, systematizing their thoughts, and leading churches. For example, the key to interpreting any biblical passage is the historical background—the background of the original language, author, recipients, situation, and ancient culture. These backgrounds are necessary for correctly interpreting a passage but are also not known or understood by most Christians.

It is not enough to merely correctly interpret a given passage; our interpretations need to be systematized—this is called systematic theology. In short, systematic theology is creating an overarching theology that governs the entire story of the Bible. It is figuring out how to allow passages to work together and which passages we will prioritize over other passages.[11] How we systematize this information directly influences how we think, talk, and what we believe about God. There is much more that can and probably should be said here, but the point is that every church has a theology, and yet probably needs a better thought-out and developed theology.

Finally, if you have ever worked with a church, you know that it is not easy. The church is like a living organism that needs careful attention and nurturing. Therefore, why would we not want people who are trained in caring for and

---

[11] For a deep dive into both biblical and systematic theology, check out my podcast and blog at thinkingtheologically.org.

leading a church congregation? This is the whole reason that seminaries and Christian universities were created.

The way the minister talks about God is at the core of developing a church's culture. If God is an angry God looking for people to punish, then a culture of fear will be cultivated. On the flip side, if the love of God displayed in Jesus is the focal point of discussions about God, then a culture of love will be cultivated. This is true not only through sermon presentation but also through all the minister's interactions in the congregation's life. How does the minister talk about God and the church in counseling sessions? How does the minister talk about God while having coffee with a member? How does the minister share God on social media?

In addressing Timothy, the young minister, Paul says that he is to "proclaim the message; be persistent whether the time is favorable or unfavorable; convince, rebuke, and encourage, with the utmost patience in teaching" (2 Tm 4:2). One of the jobs of a minister is to teach or preach the Gospel. It should be remembered that the term Gospel comes from the Greek word meaning "good news." The message preached by the minister is a message of good news. Too often, churches proclaim a message that might be news, but it is not good news. A minister must ensure that the message proclaimed is indeed good for those who hear it.

The message of the good news is found through the witness of Scripture. Paul says that "all scripture is inspired by God and is useful for teaching, for reproof, for correction, and for training in righteousness, so that everyone who belongs to God may be proficient, equipped for every good work" (2 Tm 3:16–17). The phrase "inspired by God" (gk.

θεόπνευστος, *theopneustos*) literally means "God-breathed." God's breath or Spirit (same word in Greek) is how God gives life. In the beginning, God gave life to human beings by breathing into them (Gn 2:7).

The purpose of Scripture is to breathe life into God's people. Therefore, ministers are to proclaim the Scriptures that have the power, through the Holy Spirit, to breathe life into the congregation over which they have been selected to minister. They teach, reproof, correct, and train a congregation so that they can be "equipped for every good work." The purpose of Scripture, the Holy Spirit, and the minister who proclaims the Scriptures through the power and gifting of the Holy Spirit is to equip the people of God to actively participate in God's story.

As we've discussed in this book, the church is meant to actively participate in God's story. God is in the process of transforming the world into a new creation. God will complete his mission with or without you and me. However, God has invited us to be active participants in his story. We take part in this story through the life and equipping that is breathed into us through Scripture.

This means that the primary role of a minister is not many of the things that get placed upon a minister. A minister is not primarily a counselor, though they may counsel. A minister is not a social media expert, though they may utilize social media. A minister is not primarily a decision-maker, though they need to be heavily involved in the decision-making process of the congregation. A minister is not primarily a visitor of the sick, though visiting the sick is vital to ministry. A minister is not primarily a preacher, though preaching is a must. A minister is primarily an instrument of God to breathe life into God's people so they can actively take part in God's story.

Many churches hire a minister to grow their church. There is nothing wrong with growing a church through proclaiming the Gospel to people who have never heard or obeyed. However, the primary job of a minister is not to grow a church, nor does God desire every church to be a mega-church. The job of a minister is to equip a congregation for participation in God's story. If a minister has allowed the Spirit to work through them to grow a congregation's ability and active participation in God's story, the growth in numbers is not important. However, I do believe that the more equipped and mature the spiritual life of a congregation is, the more that congregation will grow in other ways. It might not be in thousands of new members, but God will use that congregation to do amazing things.

In 1 Timothy, Paul says that Timothy should not let anyone "despise your youth, but set the believers an example in speech and conduct, in love, in faith, in purity" (1 Tm 4:12). The primary way a minister equips a church is through their actions, not their words. Relationships have more of an impact than any words a minister could utter. Almost the entire congregation will forget the words of the sermon by the time they get into the parking lot, but people will not forget how a minister made them feel.

A minister earns the right to speak to a congregation. By building a relationship with people and understanding their lives and struggles, a minister becomes a better preacher, and people's ears are better opened to their words:

a minister, first and foremost, ministers to people to equip them to become ministers themselves.

If all of this is indeed the case, then ministers play perhaps the most critical role in cultivating a church's culture. Therefore, ministers should be treated as such. It amazes me how many churches have a minister who has been educated and gifted by God to equip God's people but is not allowed by the other leadership. Ministers need a voice and a vote in all decisions of a church. Ministers must be free to make decisions about the church's ministry (e.g., staff, programs, outreach, sermons, etc.). If a church desires to cultivate a good, Spirit-powered culture, then the church must empower its minister(s) to minister.

Conclusion

If a church is to cultivate a good, Spirit-powered culture, then it begins with leadership. Not merely the particular people chosen for leadership positions, as important as this is, but also the process of selecting leaders. Leaders must be selected through a process of spiritual discernment, and their function will be dependent on this process. Leaders must be chosen based on the power and gifting of the Spirit. Leaders must understand the job and role that God has placed on them, and not try to do too much or too little. Most of all, ministers must desire and be allowed to minister.

If I could give one key to successfully unlocking the leadership process in churches, it would be this: God-chosen and Spirit-powered leaders are already leading. If you are searching for an elder, deacon, or minister, look at the people who are already filling the role unofficially. Leaders don't become leaders when they are asked, they are led and gifted by the Spirit over time to take on the official role of leading Christ's church. Therefore, they will be leading long before anyone asks them to step into an office.

If a church can succeed in the leadership process, as difficult as this may be, they will set themselves on a path to allow the Holy Spirit to cultivate a powerful culture that will propel the church into the future.

Conclusion

God's interactions with the world tell a story. This story began with God's creation of the heavens and the earth as his temple. However, Genesis 3–11 demonstrates the depths to which sin has infected God's creation. God's story to redeem his creation begins with his call of Abram (Gn 12), continues through Israel, and culminates in Jesus—God come to tabernacle among his creation (Jn 1:14). The completion of God's story will take place in the future when Jesus returns and ushers in the new heavens and new earth.

God can and will complete his story with or without you and me. However, God has invited us—those who place their allegiance in King Jesus, who are empowered by God's Spirit, and who make up the body of Christ in the church—to be active characters in this story. God desires to work out his story to redeem the creation through our broken earthly vessels. I firmly believe the primary way God does this is through our collective selves in the church.

God can and does use individuals to fulfill his purposes, but I believe, more often than not, God chooses to use the church. When discussing sports teams, people say the whole is greater than the sum of the parts. By this, they mean that a unified team is able to accomplish more than the individual players' abilities combined. Something special happens when people come together with a common goal. The same is true with the church. When Christians come together in a unified body of Christ, the whole is greater than the sum of the parts. God can and does accomplish great things through us individually, but he accomplishes even greater things through us collectively.

The power of the church body goes far beyond the collective strength of a sports team because the church has something no other group possesses—the Holy Spirit. Through the indwelling of the Holy Spirit, our churches have access to the power of God that is at work for us. The Spirit empowers us to participate in God's story and achieve things through us that are beyond our human abilities, forcing people to give glory to God.

Every church and church leader must ask, will we allow God's Spirit to work through us? Will we lead our churches in a way that is in tune with the Spirit? We do this by cultivating a church culture. Our church culture can either enable or hinder our ability to participate in God's mission and be empowered by the Spirit. God can work through a bad culture, but the more our cultures are in touch with the Spirit, the more we allow God to use us for his purposes.

This directly impacts the future of the church. Currently, the church's future looks bleak at best. The church's problem is not that God's story has failed. It is that the church has failed to cultivate good, Spirit-powered cultures. Most churches do not even realize they have a culture that needs to be cultivated. For the church to powerfully participate in God's story moving into the future, we must intentionally cultivate good, Spirit-powered church cultures.

Everything that is done or said in a church contributes to the church's culture. Nothing is too small to impact the culture and future of a church. The process, though, begins with church leaders. Church leaders must intentionally act and speak in a way that cultivates a Spirit-powered culture. They must equip the saints to participate in God's story and perpetuate the Spirit-powered culture.

For those of you who have made it to this part of the book, I pray at least some of these words were helpful for your life and the life of your church. I pray that you will be conscious of the type of culture that exists in your church and how your words and actions cultivate that culture. I pray that you will allow the Spirit to empower you to fully participate in God's story, that you will place your full faith in the hope of your future in Jesus, and that God will do things through you that no one thought possible.

I have confidence that God will do this and more. I believe the church has a bright future. I merely pray that we are a part of this future, though God's story will come to completion either way. I have confidence that a revival is just outside our grasp, attainable only by releasing control and allowing God's Spirit to guide us into the future.
God's story is only beginning. So, this is only the beginning of the church's story, too!

Appendix I

How to Craft a Vision Statement

A church's vision statement is its concentrated understanding of God's story and what it means for them to be active participants in this story. The process of crafting a vision statement begins with defining God's story: What is the overarching story? What is God doing in the world? What is the Gospel?

As developed in this book, I would define God's story as creation to new creation in light of the cross. God's story began with the creation of the heavens and the earth as his temple, and the story ends with God bringing heaven and earth back together. The story ends where it began. What makes this story go round is the life, death, burial, resurrection, and ascension of Jesus.

This story can be simplified even further by asking, what in this story is Gospel? What is the good news? Why is this story good for those who hear it? For me, the Gospel is the life, death, and resurrection of Jesus. Through these events, Jesus conquered the powers of evil that control the world and our lives. Jesus gave us hope of a new creation, with new bodies, where there will be no more pain, tears, or death. Jesus brought us into a loving relationship with the God who created us, opening the door for us to find the fullness of life through the life God created and designed for us. This is good news!

You may define the story and the Gospel differently than me, or parts of it, which is perfectly fine. The point is that you must simply and concretely define God's story, and what about this story can be considered good news. Everything in Scripture is able to breathe life into God's people, but not everything is helpful in defining a church's vision. For a church to be effective in living out a vision, it must have a simple enough concept of what God is doing that can be referred to when trying to figure out what the church should be doing. God's story and the Gospel are produced from Scripture, but it is a simplified version of the entirety of Scripture.

Once God's story and the Gospel have been defined, the church must then ask, what does it look like for us to be an active participant in this story? What does it look like for us to live out this Gospel? What are God's desires for our church? To answer these questions, a church must take an inventory of its congregation and community. Who makes up your church? What are their spiritual gifts? Are they primarily upper, middle, or lower class? Is your congregation ethnically diverse? Is your congregation theologically conservative, progressive, in the middle, or diverse?

Similar questions must be asked about a church's community. Is the community primarily upper, middle, or lower class? What is the distribution of ethnicities in the community? What are their primary occupations? What are the most successful churches in the area? Where do they stand theologically?

The way God uses a church in his story is directly related to the people God has gifted to the church and the community in which God has placed the church. A church can form a vision that is entirely faithful to God's story and the Gospel, but it can be a vision that cannot be achieved by the current gifts God has given to the church. It can be a vision that does not take into account all the people God has gifted to the church. It can be a vision that does not participate in God's worldwide story because it means nothing to the church's community. To be an active participant in God's story, a church must consider all these factors.

There is one brief side comment I would like to make. When a church does this, they will quickly figure out whether their church is a reflection of the community. If the community is ethnically diverse, but the church is primarily white, the church is not a reflection of the community. If the community is primarily lower class, but the church is all upper class, it is not a reflection of the community. I firmly believe that a church should be a reflection of the community in which God has placed it.

Once a great deal of time in prayer, discernment, and investigation has taken place to answer these questions, a church can begin crafting a vision statement. The vision statement should incorporate the church's expression of God's story and the Gospel and fit with the people God has gifted the church and the community in which God has placed the church. Let me give you a couple of examples.

I am the minister at the Lumberton Church of Christ in Lumberton, TX. I have already defined my conception of God's story and the Gospel. My church is made up mostly of middle-class white congregants with a mild diversity of theological beliefs, with most sitting somewhere toward the middle, but the church's practices are more traditional. Most of our church members grew up Christians and have been members of our church for a long time. Our community is a growing community with a growing school system. Most are also middle to upper class, and 99% of the community is white.

Therefore, our vision is to Love God, Serve People, Bless the World. Since our congregation and community are primarily believers and have been for a while, our vision is to facilitate people loving God, not just believing in God. How do we love God and desire to be part of God's story? How do we help ourselves and our community to allow the love of God shown in Jesus's death, burial, and resurrection to cause us to love God in return?

God's story and the Gospel of Jesus is a story for people. Jesus came and died as a servant, not to be served. We desire to participate in God's story and live out the Gospel by serving people. How do we take the faith of our members, which has been there for their entire lives, and put legs and feet on it? How do we take our faith out of the building and into the lives of real people in our community?

Finally, we desire to bless the world by loving God and serving people. God's story is a world-wide story. God desires to bless the entire creation by making a new heaven and new earth. We want to participate in this story. We want to allow God to use us to make the world new, even if it is just in the small part of the world in which we exist.

The second example I want to give is The Hills Church, led by senior minister Rick Atchley.[1] The Hills is a multi-campus church in the Dallas-Fort Worth area. The church is large and ethnically diverse. Its beliefs are evangelical, but many things this church does are innovative and forward-thinking.

The Hills states their mission like this: "The Hills Church exists to make and grow followers of Jesus." They say that this mission is unchanging. For The Hills, this mission directly connects to their understanding of God's story and the Gospel. God's story is to make and grow followers of Jesus, which is good news for those invited into a relationship with Jesus.

The Hills' vision is for "nations and generations because every age group and people group matters to God." This vision makes perfect sense for The Hills. It fits with their understanding of God's story and the Gospel. If God desires to make and grow followers of Jesus, then this mission is not limited to a particular group of people. Additionally, since The Hills is a large and diverse church that exists in a large and diverse city, it should be a church that actively seeks to impact the lives of all age groups and people groups because they matter to God.

The final point I want to make is that a vision can and should change. A church's definition of God's story and the Gospel does not generally change, though it can as a church grows in its understanding of God and Scripture, though these changes should not happen often or drastically.

[1] Find more information about The Hills at thehills.org.

However, as a church changes, God gifts the church different people, and as a church's community changes, so should the church's vision. There is no set amount of time that a church's vision will last. For some churches, the vision may last for a long time. For others, it might change after a few years. Regardless, a church should continuously evaluate how its vision not only lives out its definition of God's story and the Gospel but also connects to the makeup of the church and the community.

Appendix II

How to Use Social Media

I believe that every church can and should be using social media. First, social media is typically the first place a potential visitor will look before visiting your church. If you have no social media, it will appear to others that you are irrelevant and locked in the past. If your social media looks terrible, is outdated, or contains virtually no posts, you will not make a good first impression. For many, your first impression will be through social media. So make it a good one!

Second, social media is Google for the younger generations. Whereas millennials and older go to Google to find information or answers to their questions, younger generations turn to social media. Inevitably, this means that social media is where young people are looking for information and answers about religion, spirituality, and God. This makes social media a prime opportunity to reach the world with the message of the Gospel.

Third, the members of your congregation are on social media. You can put things on social media to make a good first impression on potential visitors and reach people with the Gospel, but your members will also see it. This means that social media posts can also function as a teaching opportunity for your members.

The way every church uses social media is going to look different. A large church with someone hired to run its social media accounts will be able to do much more than a small church with one staff member. However, there are still ways to utilize social media, regardless of your church's size or number of volunteers. One thing to look for is a young person who is already using all the social media apps to run the social media for you, at least under the supervision of a wise mentor.

There are many ways a church's social media may look, but here is a list of some helpful tips for utilizing social media:

1. Make sure your utilization of social media fits with your church's vision. What you put on social media should help establish and share your vision. Before beginning, meet with your leadership team and social media team to create a set of guidelines that help ensure that the church's use of social media fits with the church's   vision.

2. Be consistent. The most important aspect of utilizing social media is consistency. Everything you post doesn't have to be a perfectly edited video. It can be a short clip shot on your phone's front camera. It can be a Bible verse or information about an upcoming event. To get more views and to have a positive impact on potential guests, consistency is key.

3. Don't use too many social media sites. Find one or two that you can easily manage. Don't overextend yourself. In this same vein, remember that posts or

videos can generally be shared to multiple social media platforms. For example, a Facebook reel can also be used as a YouTube short or Instagram reel.

4. Utilize the media and content you are already creating. Churches are one of the few organizations that don't have to worry about coming up with content. Every week, you have Bible classes and sermons. There is no reason to create a ton of 'extra' new content when you are making content every week.

5. You don't have to stream. Covid made every church become a streaming church, and this is not a good thing. Your stream reflects your church's culture. If it looks bad, people will assume you have a bad culture and don't care. If you have the equipment to do a good stream, do it. If you don't, do video recordings instead and post them later. Posting a high-quality edited recording is much easier than doing a livestream.

6. If you do livestream, don't post only the live stream. Making the live stream easily accessible to people is important. However, if someone is checking out your website, social media, or YouTube channel, they typically look for the sermon, not the entire worship service. Spend a little time clipping out the sermon to increase   online   traffic.

7. Use Artificial Intelligence. In the new world of AI, you can do far more with less. For example, I use a

service called Opus Clips. Opus Clips allows me to upload an entire sermon video, and it generates social media clips in vertical format with captions. I don't have to comb through the entire video, clip, and edit myself. You can even schedule clips to post on social media straight from the website.

Bibliography

Betz, H. D. *2 Corinthians 8 and 9*. Philadelphia: Fortress Press, 1985.

Bevere, Allan R., and John Frederick. "The Letter to the Colossians." In *Dictionary of Paul and His Letters: A Compendium of Contemporary Biblical Scholarship*, edited by Scot McKnight, 239–55. Downers Grove, IL: IVP Academic, 2023.

Bland, Dave. "Background, Qualities, and Function of Elders in the Church." *Journal of Christian Studies* 2, no. 3 (September 2023): 23–40.

Brown, Jeannine K. "The Letter to the Philippians." In *Dictionary of Paul and His Letters: A Compendium of Contemporary Biblical Scholarship*, edited by Scot McKnight, 808–18. Downers Grove, IL: IVP Academic, 2023.

Bruce, F. F. *1 & 2 Thessalonians*. Word Biblical Commentary 45. Waco, TX: Word Books, 1982.

Burge, Ryan P. "Gen Z and Religion in 2021." *Religion in Public* (blog), June 15, 2022. Available at religioninpublic.blog/2022/06/15/gen-z-and-religion-in-2021/.

Byron, John. "The Letter to Philemon." In *Dictionary of Paul and His Letters: A Compendium of Contemporary Biblical Scholarship*, edited by Scot McKnight, 801–8. Downers Grove, IL: IVP Academic, 2023.

ChurchTrac. "Gen Z and Religion: How Churches Can Reach Generation Z in 2024." ChurchTrac. Available at churchtrac.com/articles.

Clear, James. *Atomic Habits: An Easy & Proven Way to Build Good Habits & Break Bad Ones.* New York: Avery, 2018.

Cousar, Charles B. *Galatians.* Interpretation: A Bible Commentary for Preaching and Teaching. Louisville, KY: Westminster John Knox Press, 2012.

deSilva, David A. *Honor, Patronage, Kinship & Purity: Unlocking New Testament Culture.* Downers Grove, IL: IVP Academic, 2000.

Dodd, Brian. "'This Is NOT A Democracy' and 5 Lessons On Creating A Winning Culture From Nick Saban's Epic Rant." *Brian Dodd on Leadership* (blog), August 22, 2021. Available at briandoddonleadership.com/2021/08/22/this-is-not-a-democracy-and-5-lessons-on-creating-a-winning-culture-from-nick-sabans-epic-rant/.

Dunn, James D. G. *Romans 1-8.* Word Biblical Commentary 38A. Dallas, TX: Word Books, 1988.

Fee, Gordon D., and Douglas Stuart. *How to Read the Bible Book by Bood: A Guided Tour.* Grand Rapids, MI: Zondervan, 2002.

Finer, Lawrence B. "Trends in Premarital Sex in the United States, 1954–2003." *Public Health Reports* 122, no. 1 (2007): 73–78.

Gaventa, Beverly Roberts. *When in Romans: An Invitation to Linger with the Gospel According to Paul.* Theological Explorations for the Church Catholic. Grand Rapids, MI: Baker Academic, 2018.

Georgi, D. *The Opponents of Paul in Second Corinthians.* Philadelphia: Fortress Press, 1986.

Gilmore, Lisa. "How Many People Go To Disney World Every Day?" *AllEars.Net* (blog), June 1, 2023. Available at allears.net/2023/06/01/how-many-people-go-to-disney-world-every-day/.

Gupta, N., and M. Bird. *Philippians*. NCBC. Cambridge: Cambridge University Press, 2020.

Guttmacher Institute. "Premarital Sex Is Nearly Universal Among Americans, And Has Been For Decades," March 1, 2016. Available at guttmacher.org/news-release/2006/premarital-sex-nearly-universal-among-americans-and-has-been-decades.

Hafemann, S. J. "Letters to the Corinthians." In *Dictionary of Paul and His Letters*, edited by Gerald F. Hawthorne, Ralph P. Martin, and Daniel G. Reid. Downers Grove, IL: InterVarsity Press, 1993.

Hays, Richard B. "Galatians." In *Acts, Introduction to Epistolary Literature, Romans, 1 & 2 Corinthians, Galatians*, vol. IX. The New Interpreter's Bible Commentary. Nashville, TN: Abingdon Press, 2015.

Hurd, J. C. *The Origin of 1 Corinthians*. London: SPCK, 1965.

Inc, Gallup. "In U.S., Childhood Churchgoing Habits Fade in Adulthood." Gallup.com, December 21, 2022. Available at news.gallup.com/poll/467354/childhood-churchgoing-habits-fade-adulthood.aspx.

Janci, Peter. "Church Sexual Abuse Statistics: Understanding the Prevalence Abuse." *Crew Janci LLP: Sexual Abuse Attorneys* (blog), May 24, 2023. Available at crewjanci.com/church-sexual-abuse-statistics/.

Jones, Jeffrey M. "U.S. Church Membership Falls Below Majority for First Time." Gallup.com, March 29, 2021.

Available at news.gallup.com/poll/341963/church-membership-falls-below-majority-first-time.aspx.

Kelso, Alicia. "Chick-Fil-A Continues to Gain Market Share While Setting Another Average Unit Volume Record." Nation's Restaurant News, April 4, 2024. Available at nrn.com/quick-service/chick-fil-continues-gain-market-share-while-setting-another-average-unit-volume-record.

Kidson, L. M. "Pastoral Epistles." In *Dictionary of Paul and His Letters: A Compendium of Contemporary Biblical Scholarship*, edited by Scot McKnight, 755–69. Downers Grove, IL: IVP Academic, 2023.

Krejcir, Richard J. "Statistics and Reasons for Church Decline." Available at churchleadership.org/?articleid=42346.

Lightfoot, J. B. "The Destination of the Epistle to the Ephesians." In *Biblical Essays*, 375–96. London: Macmillan, 1893.

Lincoln, Andrew T. *Ephesians*. Word Biblical Commentary 42. Dallas, TX: Word Books, 1990.

Lindner, Jannik. "Gen Z Religion Statistics And Trends in 2024 • Gitnux." Available at gitnux.org/gen-z-religion-statistics/.

Long, Thomas G. *The Witness of Preaching*. Second Edition. Louisville, KY: Westminster John Knox Press, 2005.

Longenecker, Richard N. *Galatians*. Word Biblical Commentary 41. Dallas, TX: Word Books, 1990.

MacroTrends. "McDonald's Revenue 2010-2024." Available at macrotrends.net/stocks/charts/MCD/mcdonalds/revenue#.

Matthews, V. H. "Family Relationships." In *Dictionary of the Old Testament: Pentateuch*, edited by Alexander T. Desmond and David W. Baker. Downers Grove, IL: InterVarsity Press, 2003.

McCain, Abby. "22 McDonald's Statistics [2023]: Restaurant Counts, Facts, And Trends." *Zippia* (blog), March 21, 2023. Available at zippia.com/advice/mcdonalds-statistics/.

McKnight, Scot. *A Church Called Tov: Forming a Goodness Culture That Resists Abuses of Power and Promotes Healing.* Carol Stream, IL: Tyndale Elevate, 2020.

———. "The Letter to the Romans." In *Dictionary of Paul and His Letters: A Compendium of Contemporary Biblical Scholarship*, edited by Scot McKnight, 930–43. Downers Grove, IL: IVP Academic, 2023.

———. *Pastor Paul: Nurturing a Culture of Christoformity in the Church.* Grand Rapids, MI: Brazos Press, 2019.

Meneo, Ron. "Catholic Church Priest Abuse | Sexual Abuse Scandal & Cover-Up." AbuseLawsuit.com, May 11, 2023. Available at abuselawsuit.com/church-sex-abuse/.

O'Brien, Peter Thomas. "The Letter to the Colossians." In *Dictionary of Paul and His Letters*, edited by Gerald F. Hawthorne, Ralph P. Martin, and Daniel G. Reid. Downers Grove, IL: InterVarsity Press, 1993.

Oden, Thomas C. *Classical Pastoral Care*, vols. 1–4. New York: Crossroad, 1987.

Porter, Stanley E. *The Letter to the Romans: A Linguistic and Literary Commentary.* New Testament Monographs 37. Sheffield: Sheffield Phoenix Press, 2015.

Richards, E. Randolph, and Brandon O'Brien. *Misreading Scripture with Western Eyes*. Downers Grove, IL: InterVarsity Press, 2013.

Sampley, Paul J. "1 & 2 Corinthians." In *Acts, Introduction to Epistolary Literature, Romans, 1 & 2 Corinthians, Galatians*, vol. IX. The New Interpreter's Bible Commentary. Nashville, TN: Abingdon Press, 2015.

Sensing, Tim, ed. *The Effective Practice of Ministry*. Abilene, TX: Abilene Christian University Press, 2013.

Steinke, Peter L. "Congregational Leadership in Anxious Times: Being Calm and Courageous No Matter What." Lanham, MD: Rowman & Littlefield, 2006.

Strait, Drew. "Peace, Reconciliation." In *Dictionary of Paul and His Letters: A Compendium of Contemporary Biblical Scholarship*, edited by Scot McKnight, 792–96. Downers Grove, IL: IVP Academic, 2023.

Walton, John H. *The Lost World of Genesis One*, vol. 2. Ancient Cosmology and the Origins Debate. Downers Grove, IL: IVP Academic, 2009.

Watson, Duane F. "Roman Social Classes." In *Dictionary of New Testament Background: A Compendium of Biblical Scholarship*, edited by Stanley E. Porter and Craig A. Evans, 99–104. Downers Grove, IL: InterVarsity Press, 2000.

Wenham, Gordon J. *Genesis 1-15*. Word Biblical Commentary 1. Waco, TX: Word Books, 1987.

Willimon, William H. *Pastor: The Theology and Practice of Ordained Ministry*. Nashville, TN: Abingdon Press, 2002.

Wright, N. T. *Paul and His Letter to the Ephesians*. Logos Mobile Education. Waukesha, WI: The Wisconsin Center for Christian Study, 2019.

———. "Paul and His Letter to the Philippians: Small Group Edition." Online Course, Udemy, n.d.

———. "Romans." In *Acts, Introduction to Epistolary Literature, Romans, 1 & 2 Corinthians, Galatians*, vol. IX. The New Interpreter's Bible Commentary. Nashville, TN: Abingdon Press, 2015.

———. *Scripture and the Authority of God: How to Read the Bible Today*. New York: HarperOne, 2013.